Comments on *Mole Under the Fence: Conversations with Roland Walls*

'Here at last in this book is the opportunity for Roland Walls' witness to be better known – a genuine theologian, a genuine monastic, something approaching a "fool for Christ" in the Eastern Orthodox sense, a man belonging to the wholeness of the Catholic Church in a rare way. We are very fortunate indeed to have this wonderful introduction to such a great and joyful friend of God.' **Rowan Williams, Archbishop of Canterbury**

'Roland Walls came to see me shortly after I was ordained archbishop – quite simply to promise obedience to me as his new bishop and to ask what I wanted him to do as a priest of the archdiocese! His deep spirituality and even greater humility led me to revere him greatly during my time as archbishop, knowing, as I did, of the countless numbers who sought his advice and prayers at Roslin. My hope is that this book will reveal more of Roland's spirituality and insights to a much wider audience.' **Keith Patrick Cardinal O'Brien, Archbishop of St Andrews and Edinburgh**

'This book is a treasure. For all who would like to have their life and their faith illuminated by the wisdom and hilarity of Roland Walls, it provides the unmistakable sound of his conversation. For any who have not known him, it offers an encounter with one of the liveliest and most creative theological minds of his generation. We owe Ron Ferguson a great debt of gratitude for presenting us with this written enactment of Roland Walls at work.' **Very Rev. Dr John Miller, Castlemilk East Parish Church**

'This book deserves to   Roland
Walls is known and lov   on. Talks
he gave to us as undergi   memory.
Anecdotes deriving fron   Scotland
are often repeated. Wha   and has
circulated freely by word of mouth, has now been preserved. The
book captures the spirit of Roland's conversational style, it offers

us the depth and humour of his perceptions, it brings him before us in an authentic way, and it introduces us to some of those with whom he shared his journey of faith. Ron Ferguson has done us all a great service in enabling us to meet with him through these pages.' **The Rt Rev. Brian Smith, Bishop of Edinburgh**

'Roland Walls has always surprised and challenged those who encounter him to imaginative new ways of seeing, understanding and living the love of God. At his simple table, you might sit next to a bishop or an ex-con; in his inspirational classes, you were led to hold heart and head together. Ron Ferguson has wonderfully captured the essence of this extraordinary man.' **Rev. Alison Newell, Ignatian Spirituality Centre, Glasgow**

'I was a philosophy student at Edinburgh from 1967 to 1971 and was attached to the Student Christian Movement. Several of us in the SCM used to go regularly to hear Roland preach at evensong at Roslin.

He is one of the two or three strongest Christian influences on me. He opened my eyes. Most of the perspectives I still hold were first discussed with Roland or transmitted from him in one way or another. He helped both Morag and me immensely. It was utterly natural to ask Roland to marry us at Roslin later.

I needed him as part of my growing up and disengagement from my father [*Professor T. F. Torrance, one of the world's leading theologians*]. Roland supplied common sense – both theological and human – as much as he could, to my father. He was one of the very few people who used to tease him.

He once told me a wonderful story. He had made up a series of little cards, probably filing cards, each of which had a quotation from Calvin or from Augustine on them. The quotations were not attributed. He challenged my father to take the test. My father loved Roland and loved a challenge, and took it on gamely. I think he got something like eight out of ten. I remember Roland said to him something like: "Tom, that's not at all bad. That's an alpha minus mark! You'll make a theologian yet."' **Very Rev. Professor Iain R. Torrance, President, Princeton Theological Seminary, New Jersey**

MOLE UNDER THE FENCE

CONVERSATIONS WITH ROLAND WALLS

RON FERGUSON
with Mark Chater

Foreword by Rowan Williams

SAINT ANDREW PRESS
Edinburgh

First published in 2006 by
SAINT ANDREW PRESS
121 George Street, Edinburgh EH2 4YN

Copyright © Ron Ferguson and Mark Chater, 2006

ISBN 10-digit: 0 7152 0832 2
ISBN 13-digit: 978 0 7152 0832 8

British Library Cataloguing in Publication Data
A catalogue record for this book is available from the British Library.

Typeset by Waverley Typesetters in 11½ on 13½pt Sabon
Printed and bound by Creative Print & Design, Wales

CONTENTS

FOREWORD

Writers and publishers sometimes talk about a 'word-of-mouth bestseller' – a book that isn't intensively promoted and advertised but simply and steadily wins recognition because it says things that no other book does. And sooner or later, that recognition becomes public, and more people are able to share the secret.

It's tempting to think that something a bit like that operates in the sphere of recognising authoritative figures in the world of Christian witness and teaching. There are the familiar names and the row of books – but there are also the ones who don't write, don't broadcast, and just get on with it. But here, too, the secret will sooner or later get out.

Roland Walls has a good case for being the equivalent of a word-of-mouth bestseller – a man who has never sought the limelight or played any kind of professional clerical or theological games. If that suggests a withdrawn ascetic, the pages that follow will soon correct any such idea; but he has simply refused to do expected and conventional things in and for Christ's Church and so has had all the more extraordinary an effect on those who have been lucky enough to know him. He has brought God so vividly alive to so many; the retreat I heard him give nearly thirty years ago is still immediate to my mind, one of the things I turn back to when faith seems full of struggle and unclarity – and I don't think I'm the only one to be able to say so.

Here at last in this book is the opportunity for his witness to be better known – a genuine theologian, a genuine monastic, something approaching a 'fool for Christ' in the Eastern Orthodox sense, a man belonging to the wholeness of the Catholic Church in a rare way. We are very fortunate indeed to have this wonderful introduction to such a great and joyful friend of God.

ROWAN WILLIAMS
Archbishop of Canterbury
February 2006

ACKNOWLEDGEMENTS

I would like to thank Dr Mark Chater, Reader in Education at Bishop Grosseteste College, Lincoln, for all his help. Mark had also tape-recorded some conversations with Roland Walls, and generously agreed that parts of his material could be incorporated within the text. Not only that, but also Mark has given me enthusiastic encouragement and support in this task. Without him, this manuscript might not have seen the light of day.

Mark's material has been interwoven into the completed text. We both felt that from the reader's point of view it did not matter who had asked which question, so there are no indications in the text – though there are occasional points at which the identity of the questioner will be obvious. The questions or comments are designed to prompt Roland rather than to effect a Paxmanesque interrogation. The object of the exercise was to introduce readers to Roland Walls' thinking in his favoured manner, namely conversation.

The process of editing the text was illuminating. I was well aware, of course, of the difference between oral and written material, but I had not realised the extent of that difference. A simple transcription dumped on to the page would have tested the patience of even the most well-disposed reader. I have taken the liberty of eliminating most of the 'as it weres' and 'I means' which mark most conversational styles but which are irritating, I mean, in cold print, as it were. Not only that, but also Roland's engagingly discursive style meant that sentences would sometimes change gear halfway through and never make it back to home base. In the editorial process, I have tried to remain true to his intentions while producing a written text which could be read without resort to a cold compress.

Most of the original conversations had chosen themes, but would sometimes spiral unexpectedly into other territory. I have, in the interests of overall coherence, taken the liberty of corralling some of the diverse material and placing it into its main theme chapters. Oral conversation happens without benefit of full stops, colons and semicolons, therefore sentence-structure decisions have had to be made all the way through.

All this is a way of saying that I haven't treated Roland's *ipsa verba* as the oral equivalent of sacred scripture. The result, I hope, is true to Roland's style and intentions while at the same time being a very readable text. Christianity abounds in Capital Letters, too many of which can induce migraine; I have tried to cut down on the number. Anyway, any failings of editorial judgement are mine alone.

I would like to thank Roland Walls for his patience in answering the questions put to him, and to thank Brother John Halsey and Sister Patty Burgess for their kindness and support.

Throughout its forty years of existence, the Community of the Transfiguration has eschewed publicity, making a conscious decision to work in modest and low-profile ways. I should point out that the initiative for this book came from myself and not from the Community, and therefore should not be seen as a product of the Community. While Roland, John and Patty have corrected errors in the text and have given me their warm blessing, the responsibility for the project is entirely mine. It should also be made clear that the Community of the Transfiguration does not have the resources, human or financial, to enter into correspondence about their life and work or to receive visitors as a result of the publication of this book.

I am personally indebted to Rowan Williams, Archbishop of Canterbury, not only for taking the time in the midst of a very demanding schedule to pen such a typically gracious and generous foreword, but also for so many illuminating theological reflections which continue to sustain my own faith journey.

Warm thanks, too, to Sandra Leslie and Moira Irvine for their work in the transcription of the oral material. Their task was made more difficult by Roland's continual lighting of his pipe and by his frequent collapses into laughter. As a reminder of this hilarity, I have occasionally made reference to the laughter; readers are invited to hear it at frequent intervals as they 'listen' to the text.

INTRODUCTION

The rumbling bus takes me from the centre of Edinburgh on a southward trajectory. Beyond the city boundary, we are in attractive, rolling countryside heading towards Dalkeith, then further through the Esk Valley by way of old mining villages such as Lasswade, Loanhead and Bilston. Forty minutes after leaving the capital, I alight in Main Street, Roslin.

People, some with transatlantic accents, stop me in the village street. Can you point us in the direction of Rosslyn Chapel? Sure. The visitors, clutching copies of Dan Brown's cult novel, *The Da Vinci Code*, are in search of the ancient Holy Grail. The book, which has sold a staggering 20 million copies worldwide, has now been made into a blockbuster Hollywood film, starring Tom Hanks. For those who have spent the last two years living in a cave, let me explain that *The Da Vinci Code* is a religious detective story. It begins with the murder of the curator of a French museum who has been killed in order to keep secret the location of a vastly important religious relic hidden for centuries.

Where does Scotland come in? Cue Rosslyn Chapel. (Rosslyn and Roslin are simply variant spellings of the same place name.) Founded in 1446 by Sir William St Clair, a prince of Orkney, the chapel has an association with the Knights Templar, an organisation formed in the twelfth century to protect pilgrims travelling to the Holy Land. It has been speculated that their treasure, including the legendary Holy Grail – often identified as the goblet used by Christ in the Last Supper – lies somewhere in Rosslyn Chapel's crypt.

So far, all good material for a fast-moving potboiler. But what has caused most jumping up and down is *The Da Vinci Code*'s assertion that the Christian Church has conspired for centuries to hide evidence that Jesus was a mere mortal. He apparently married Mary Magdalene and had children whose descendants now live in France. The central claim Brown's novel makes about Christianity is that 'almost everything our fathers taught us about Christ is false'.

The reason why *The Da Vinci Code* has moved from an airport best-seller to become an international cult book is that many of its readers believe it to be gospel truth. Its inflated marketing hype claims that the book undermines the historic foundations of the Christian Church, no less. So author, publisher and Hollywood have united in pursuit of a more modern holy grail: money. Lots and lots of it. The movie will gross millions. And the trustees of Rosslyn Chapel have a very handsome sum for their trouble.

There are now 'Da Vinci Code' tours which take American and European visitors to all of the sites mentioned in the book. Pilgrims can walk in the footsteps not just of Jesus and Mary Magdalene, but also of handsome hunk Tom Hanks! When Hollywood meets murder, mystery and delicious religious conspiracy theory, the cash registers go into overdrive. Thus it is that a quiet former mining village has been invaded from both outer and inner space.

What to make of all this? First of all, *The Da Vinci Code* is a novel. A piece of fiction. Dan Brown has been cleverly coy about this. Coached by his marketing team, he says that it's fiction, but on the other hand, he's done his homework, and …

Well, what about Brown's 'scholarship'? It's third-rate baloney dressed up as academic research. Based on rumours, mistranslations of words and implausible leaps, it ranks alongside Oor Wullie and the Broons as historical material. The notion that Jesus married Mary Magdalene – did they have a white wedding? – rests on no credible evidence whatsoever.

The Da Vinci Code works fine as a pacey page-turner, but as theology it is junk food for the mind. The trouble is that the printed word has a certain authority: if something appears in print, it must be true. Therefore the Jesus and Mary Magdalene family become like Maw, Paw and the weans, with descendants still living in France. Jacques Chirac, perhaps? Any more of this stuff and you could end up a gibbering wreck. Why not also insist that the Apostle Paul had a wooden leg and a black gay lover? Or that Saint Peter was a transvestite nightclub singer? In a world of crazed conspiracy theories, fuelled by the Internet, everything becomes believable. When people believe in nothing, they end up believing in anything. Whatever cannot be disproved becomes truth.

As I look around the dank building, I feel uncomfortable. There is something about Rosslyn Chapel which gives me the creeps, and I'm glad to leave. But the chapel has not been my principal reason for coming to Roslin; nor am I here to visit the famed Roslin Institute, the leading centre for animal biotechnology where Dolly the Sheep made her debut on earth, and which could yet be a centre for the study of the cloning of human embryos. More shivers down the spine.

No, my pilgrimage is of a different nature. My feet take me, as they have done many times before, along Manse Road in the village. I come to an unprepossessing garden, and go in through the gate. Before me is a slightly dilapidated building – a former miners' welfare institute – and beyond that there is a silent enclosure which contains six simple huts. I am at the home of the Community of the Transfiguration, and I am here to have lunch with its founder, Father Roland Walls. This unhyped experiment in Christian living is as far from *The Da Vinci Code* as it gets (though, curiously, Roland Walls was himself at one stage priest-in-charge of that same Rosslyn Chapel).

Many people have beaten a path to this unostentatious, deliberately unpublicised place over the years. Lots have come with tears to shed, shelter to be sought, guidance to be asked for, words of forgiveness to be heard, or questions to be asked. Some are academics, others clerics of many denominations. More than a few have had a vocation initiated or shaped here. Lots are ordinary seekers, or desperate people facing a life crisis. Some are mentally ill.

This tiny, vulnerable community is an arena of healing, hope and inspiration out of all proportion to its size or resources. It features in no celebrity journals, and is to be found on no international tourist trails; yet word of mouth has made it respected within a large, amorphous, unorganised network. It is a community whose future probably lies not in physical continuity but solely in its influence on many people.

I am here, as I have been several times, with my tape recorder. I have been recording conversations with Roland Walls because I believe that this former Anglican priest and Cambridge don-turned-monk-turned-Roman Catholic priest is a man with unfashionable but illuminating things to say to our times. Unsurprisingly, he has been asked on several occasions to write articles or books, but has refused.

'I can't be bothered to write all this stuff up,' he says. 'I'm a talker, I'm not a writer, I know that. My compression when I write becomes unintelligible. It always has to be unpacked and annotated and it really is absolutely appalling. So I can't do it. But if anybody wants to use anything, lying around, of what I've said, that's quite a different matter.'

I first encountered Roland Walls when I was a student at New College in the University of Edinburgh in the late 1960s, and he was on the Faculty of Divinity as a lecturer in Christian Dogmatics. His engaging, unconventional style made an immediate impact on his students. It was obvious that, while he was serious about his subject, he did not take himself seriously at all. His lectures and tutorials were punctuated by laughter as he considered the preposterousness of the Church in general, and of himself in particular.

It was not that Roland Walls didn't respect the Church – indeed, he could be described as a High Churchman – but he was possessed of a highly developed sense of the absurd. He was passionate about Jesus Christ as the revelation of God, and believed deeply that the Church itself was the main vehicle of that revelation – not for him the view that 'almost everything our fathers taught us about Christ is false' – but that did not stop him sending up the Church of Christ in its more absurd and pretentious manifestations. He reminded me of Søren Kierkegaard's wise admonition: Relate yourself absolutely to the absolute and relatively to the relative. That is to say, keep focused on the heart of the matter and hang loose to the rest.

I was one of a group of students who were sceptical about dogmatic theology, and we really went after Roland. When he said that his starting point – in company with Karl Barth – was John's gospel, chapter 1, verse 14, *And the Word became flesh and dwelt among us*, we would try to pin him to the lecture-room wall. Why that particular starting point, and not the more reticent Jesus of the first three gospels? How could he justify his starting point? Why, why, why?

Roland enjoyed the cut and thrust, even when he couldn't answer all our questions. We gave him a hard time, but we loved him. For me, what shone through the man was a transparent spirituality – how he hates that word! – and a passion for justice. His often uproarious and anarchic style masked an acute theological mind. He had gained a first-class honours *cum laude* degree in New Testament from Cambridge, on the strength of which he had been elected to the International New Testament Studies Association and offered a fellowship at Corpus Christi College, Cambridge. He played the clown, but he was no fool.

The conversations in this book will convey much about Roland's life and teachings, but here are some biographical clues to set the scene. Brought up in very humble circumstances in the Isle of Wight, the young Roland Walls, who had been greatly inspired by the example of two local Church of England clerics and also by French Benedictine monks at the local Quarr Abbey, decided at the age of 14 that he wanted to be a priest. He went to a junior seminary run by the Society of the Sacred Mission at Kelham, where the founder of SSM, the redoubtable Father Herbert Kelly, was still teaching. (Roland delights in telling of his first visit to the college and monastery, which was near Nottingham. Somehow he arrived late and missed evening chapel, which he was meant to be at. He stood uncertainly near the closed doors of the chapel, which opened into the cloisters where he was dithering. He heard the sound of solemn worship in full swing; and, as he was wondering what to do, another door further along opened, and against the light which flowed from it he could see a monkish figure standing holding something. An imperious voice called: 'Hey you, come here and do something useful'. Roland hurried forward, and the old man thrust into his hands a huge, rather full chamber pot – and, once Roland had hold of it, the door closed and the figure vanished. What on earth should he do? At that moment, the chapel doors opened and the entire college processed out past Roland, gazing in amazement at him and the strange vessel in his hands! Later, one of Roland's tasks was to look after Father Kelly near the end of his mortal days. Roland was told he had to go into Kelly's bedroom in the morning, open up the blinds and see to his charge's needs. On the first morning, Roland entered, passed the recumbent figure on the bed, headed for the blinds and let them up with a snap. He turned and looked round, wondering what to do next. The figure on the pillow had raised his hands to either side of his head and was lying apparently in some kind of trance. 'My goodness!' thought Roland, 'he's having a vision!' He gazed at the old man, stupefied. Suddenly a severe voice spoke from the pillow: 'Hairbrushes, you fool!' Roland often described Father Kelly as the greatest teacher he ever had – a Barthian before Barth, who taught him 'the difference between faith and religion'.)

After ordination to the priesthood in 1941, Roland was asked to work with the Kelham Fathers in Sheffield. Four years later, he was sent by the SSM to study at Cambridge, and he eventually became Dean of the Chapel and lecturer in the Faculty of Divinity. In 1958, he became Canon of Sheffield Cathedral, and was much involved with the experimental Sheffield Industrial Mission. The SIM project, which gained a great deal of national attention, involved working in new and radical ways with steelworkers and coalminers in the area. Roland, who was very much influenced by the theology of Dietrich Bonhoeffer, had a big impact on many of the students who came to learn from the work of the Mission.

So why Scotland? That is, in part, the subject of this book. Suffice it to say for now that, in 1962, Canon Walls became priest-in-charge of Rosslyn Chapel, which was then a quiet and largely unattended small cathedral in a field. And this sophisticated theologian came to Roslin as the result of reading a notice on the guard's van of a train in Leeds. It was this bizarre step of faith which led eventually to the formation of the Community of the Transfiguration.

Let me sketch in a little bit about that venture in order to provide further historical context for the conversations which follow. The Roslin community started life as 'The Fraternity of the Transfiguration' on 6 August – the

Feast Day of the Transfiguration – 1965, when Kenneth Carey, Scottish Episcopal Bishop of Edinburgh, took the 'promises' of three men – Roland Walls, John Halsey and Robert Haslam – in Rosslyn Chapel. The community was an ecumenical venture from the start. Its Rule stated: 'Let your form of life and engagements be open to all whom God shall call to it since it is inspired not by any particular church tradition but by the gospel and the Lord of the gospel and the tradition of the universal Church'.

The minimalist structure of the community reflected this ecumenical dimension. Like other religious communities, it had an official Visitor, the first being the Rev. Duncan Finlayson, Principal of St Colm's College, Edinburgh, who was both amused and proud to be the first Church of Scotland Visitor to a professed community since the Reformation. The three community members had to tell the Visitor what to do, but the man who was one of the finest and far-seeing Kirk ministers of his generation relished the task.

What were the earliest influences on the fledgling community? In shorthand terms – and not necessarily in order of importance – they were as follows. First, the Anglican tradition, represented by its first three members. Second, the Sheffield Industrial Mission and the worker-priest movement. Third, the Taizé Community in France, a pioneering ecumenical community of Protestant and Catholic brothers founded by the inspirational Brother Roger Schultz (who was so tragically murdered at the age of 90 on 16 August 2005). Taizé has been a place of pilgrimage for seekers – especially young people – for more than half a century, and its worship has influenced many churches. Fourth, the Little Brothers of Jesus, founded by that giant of desert spirituality, Brother Charles de Foucauld. His little communities still live under a rule of poverty and serve in the contemporary 'deserts' of inner-city struggle in several continents. Fifth, the ecumenical Iona Community, founded by the charismatic George MacLeod, whose vision was to rebuild the ruins of the living quarters of Iona's medieval abbey and to train young clerics for service in the tough urban areas of Britain. Iona, like Taizé, remains an important centre of European pilgrimage. Sixth, the Kirk, Scotland's national church, Presbyterian in its organisation and disciplines. Seventh, the Roman Catholic Church, particularly its Cistercian spirituality. Soon after Roland came to Roslin, he met Dom. Columban Mulcahy, the abbot at Nunraw in nearby Haddington, who gave this Anglican priest tremendous encouragement and support.

Roland Walls had joined the Faculty of Divinity at Edinburgh University in 1963. When the position in the New College Dogmatics department was offered to him, he was hesitant about accepting, since his speciality was New Testament studies, not Dogmatics. He was approached about the job during a coffee break at New College by the Principal, Professor J. H. S. Burleigh. When Roland was diffident, Burleigh summoned him to a quiet corner and said to him: 'A thing you and I know, which many don't, is that any university lectureship in humanities can be picked up in a few months by anyone sufficiently intelligent'. The Primus of the Scottish Episcopal Church, Francis Moncrieff, told Roland he must seize the opportunity – membership of the staff of New College had never hitherto been available to Anglicans (nor, of course, Roman Catholics). So Roland had to do a crash course in patristic studies, Calvin's *Institutes* and the twelve volumes of Karl Barth's *Church Dogmatics*.

Brother John Halsey, a worker-priest, was employed as a miner at the Roslin pit until it closed in 1969 – he was later to work in a local car bodyshop garage – and then moved into the Edinburgh Cyrenians, sharing in their care for the homeless and the dispossessed. He lived there during the week, returning to Roslin most weekends when there wasn't a crisis at the Cyrenians.

The first person to join the original three members was Neil Russell, a profoundly holy man who had been Bishop of Zanzibar. He was resident in Roslin from 1968 until 1981, when he was invited to return to Africa 'to lay his bones in his beloved Africa'. He died there in 1984.

Patty Burgess, a widow, became associated with the community in the late 1960s and soon became a surrogate mother in the Cyrenians, coming in once a week to collect an enormous amount of appalling washing and taking it to the 'steamie' up the road. Patty joined the Roslin community in 1972, causing the Fraternity to change its name to the Community of the Transfiguration. Patty started in a flat in Loanhead, but three years later moved to Roslin to fill a gap there while John and Roland were away. After their return, partly because of the logistics of living together in such a small space with primitive facilities, Patty moved back to the Loanhead flat, and a few women tested their vocation with her.

John Halsey withdrew from the work with the Cyrenians following a decision by the Community of the Transfiguration to be less activity-orientated. The members agreed that they needed to be together more and 'wait on the Lord'. They weren't given long to wait, as they were almost immediately overrun by hippies who appeared from such disparate corners as Kathmandu, Glastonbury and Findhorn. The Community had also been developing contacts with the Tibetan Buddhists at Samye Ling, in the Scottish Borders.

In the early 1970s, with the Roslin-based community being overwhelmed by visitors, a plan was devised with George Douglas, dean of the cathedral at Millport on the island of Cumbrae, and Bishop Richard Wimbush, the Diocesan for Cumbrae, to establish on the land around the cathedral an enclosure of four hut cells and a hut chapel, which would be a base for training and formation for aspiring new members of the Community of the Transfiguration. It would also provide space for those of the hippies who wanted to establish their own ashram. The extensive grounds were in a state of rampant overgrown decay and thus very suitable for the work of reclamation and cultivation – work to be shared by the Roslin brothers with the ashram members. Roland went to Millport every weekend, being briefed by Brother John, who met his ferry on Friday afternoons. The ashram community fell apart and ended in October 1971. Meanwhile, at Roslin during this time, several New College postgraduate students were living in community. The activities at both Roslin and Cumbrae were very influential for a number of students.

In 1972, Dave Brett, leader of Youth with a Mission, which was looking for a base in Scotland, moved to Cumbrae, where he stayed for nearly three years. Young, evangelical and charismatic, the group established an immediate rapport with Roland and arranged for him to teach courses on the Bible and the Psalms in his vacations from New College. In 1974, Roland Walls retired from university teaching. Many former students who had been affected by his ministry came to Roslin and Cumbrae to see him. The Community, which has rarely had more than four permanent members, continued to play host to people down on their luck, some with mental problems, and to clerics of all denominations. Some came simply to find a place of prayerful silence in the enclosure at Roslin.

When YWAM moved out of Cumbrae in 1975, their place was taken by the Community of Celebration. It had been founded by Graham Polkingham, a priest in the US Episcopal Church who was a leader of the burgeoning charismatic movement. When they arrived on Cumbrae, the Community of Celebration rather curiously regarded the tiny Roslin brotherhood as a threat. Roland and company felt the island was too small for both groups, so they withdrew from Cumbrae, apart from a cottage which they had acquired in 1972 and continued to use for retreat. In 1977, however, a member of the Community of Celebration who was studying under Roland Walls at New College persuaded his peers to invite Roland to speak to them. From 1977 until they left the island in 1985, the Roslin community developed a strong relationship with many members of the Community of Celebration.

The most dramatic happening within the Community of the Transfiguration came in 1981 when Roland Walls was received into the Roman Catholic Church, becoming a priest two years later. Roland, who had found himself drawn to Roman Catholicism for some time – the reasons are explained in these conversations – told me later that he saw the move as 'a sign of contradiction'. It meant that the pain of the separation of the Christian churches in Scotland became incarnated within this small and vulnerable community. Mass and Holy Communion became points of painful exclusion rather than of unity, right in the heart of this tiny ecumenical enterprise. Roland's decision was entirely supported by the group, who felt it right that they should live with the hard realities of ecclesiastical separation.

The move produced shock waves within church circles, especially among Roland's friends and admirers in the Church of England. However, Roland was particularly delighted to receive a postcard from the eminent Anglican theologian and patristics scholar, Professor Henry Chadwick, saying: 'We don't feel you have left us – we are glad to have a mole under the fence!' Roland delightedly embraced this notion, telling me that it meant 'going round the subterranean passages, which are enormously complex, and picking up bits and pieces, and digging a way through – some people say undermining! – the foundations'.

The Roslin group forged strong links with L'Arche Community, which has provided havens for many people with learning and physical disabilities in more than 100 communities in nearly thirty countries. The philosophy of L'Arche can be summed up in the words of its visionary founder, Jean Vanier: 'Can we reasonably have a dream of a world where people, whatever their race, religion, culture, abilities or disabilities, can find a place and reveal their gifts?' Vanier came to Roslin to visit the Community of the

Transfiguration and found its spirit to be entirely congenial. Edinburgh L'Arche Community was conceived at a prayer gathering in Roslin in 1986 and started up in 1991.

In 1989, the Community reviewed its identity and relationship to other communities, especially in the light of Brother Jonathan Jamal's situation. Jonathan had joined the Community of the Transfiguration in 1981, and, after periods as a postulant and then novice, he was solemnly professed in 1989. Because he was so much younger than the others, the Community was concerned about his future security. After full consideration, the Community of the Transfiguration came under the Benedictine Rule. In 1995, they transferred to the Franciscan family, and are now designated 'Franciscan hermits of the Transfiguration'. Jonathan subsequently moved on.

It only takes a few minutes in the company of Roland Walls to know why he has been a guru – another word he hates – for so many. The mole under the fence is both subversive and engaging. This holy maverick has the power to unsettle as well as to inspire. He is as unconventional as he is orthodox. He described himself to me as 'a Nicene radical', believing that the great orthodox Christian creed is utterly transformative in its implications. He is a one-off individual who acknowledges that he has to struggle all the time with his self-wilfulness; yet he is a community man who believes in solidarity. He is obedient to a Church which he sends up uproariously.

Indeed, Roland Walls is a holy man who laughs all the time. And, if you met him in the street, you might slip him fifty pence for a cup of tea. He looks like, well, a tramp – a dosser who finds God in the most unexpected places. The following story of his will give a little flavour:

On 2 March 1982, Professor James Torrance of Aberdeen University, my host during three days there, asked me to go to the station to meet his wife Mary off the 4:30 train. I was down in Union Street by four o'clock, so I used the time to go to the Catholic cathedral, just off Union Street, and say a few prayers. When I came out of the cathedral, I noticed a little plaque of St Francis in wood, about two feet by eight inches, rather nice, let into the plaster of the wall. I said a little prayer I always say when I see an icon of St Francis – 'Lord, get me a centimetre or two very slowly towards imitating the life of this dear man'. It was a quarter past four, and I thought I'd have a cup of tea. I couldn't find a cup of tea at less than twenty-seven pence until I found a little place called 'Lite Bite', which sold tea at seventeen pence, so I went in. The whole place was pink – pink cups and saucers, pink tables, pink mirrors, pink waitresses, pink everything. Hideous place. And I noticed, when I got in there, that everybody was embarrassed. Highly embarrassed, either sniggering, or whispering to one another and looking one way, and that was towards a poor man, aged about 50, in a dirty old mac and torn green wellies. And he was so lonely, he was having an animated conversation with himself in one of these pink mirrors. I couldn't believe there was nobody between him and the mirror. But it was so.

Well, being the good Christian that I am, and being a Catholic priest, I thought I would do some good. So I took my tea and went to his table, but then of course, all eyes were turned on me, and I was embarrassed, because I couldn't get him away from his conversation with himself – until I put out my hand and touched his arm, and said: 'How are you getting on?' He looked away from the mirror, and he says to me: 'You don't need to talk to me. I'm a nobody.' He shouted this out so everybody could hear. And I, again with the kind of self-deception one has in one's priestly ministry, said to him: 'Well, I suppose when all the chips are down, I'm a nobody too'. At this, he turned away from the mirror, and he says to me: 'Now, if you're a nobody, and only if you're a nobody, I'll tell you something. If you're not a nobody, you won't understand what I'm talking about.' Still, me with my superiority, still thinking I was on a level far above him and I was helping him, I said: 'Yes, you tell me something'. He says: 'God made all this'. He wasn't standing by Mount Pleasant, he was sitting in the Lite Bite café, which to my mind was a horror. He said: 'God made all this'. I still humoured him, because I said back: 'Yes, that's a marvellous thought, isn't it?'

Then he said to me something that turned the whole table 180 degrees, and I was on the floor, and he was helping me. He said to me: 'I'll tell you another thing. God doesn't want us to strut around like peacocks. His son, his blessed son, bowed low beneath the cross.' Ooh my God, who was there before me? Was it an angel? St Francis? Christ? Goodness knows. Then he said to me: 'Now I'm going to ask you a question'. 'Right,' I said, 'You ask me a question.' All the café still listening to all this. 'What's the greatest miracle in the world?' I said: 'I think the resurrection of Jesus Christ from the dead was the greatest miracle in the world'. 'Yes yes, that was quite a great miracle, quite a great miracle, but it wasn't the biggest.' 'Well, you tell me,' I said, 'you tell me what's the greatest miracle in the world.' 'God himself', he said.

Time was up now, so I was out in the street. And I thought to myself: what he's just told me are three parts of the four parts of the first revelation of Julian of Norwich. God made everything from the size of a hazelnut; God in his passion, with the crown of thorns pressed on his head; and God the blessed Trinity. And I was disappointed because he hadn't said anything about the fourth bit of the first revelation, that was the appearance of the Blessed Mother of God to Julian. And then I thought to myself: he has! He asked me if I was a nobody. He said if I wasn't a nobody, I wouldn't understand any of it. He was talking about the nobody-ness of the Mother of God.

So I went down to the station and met Mary off the train. She says: '*What's* happened to you?' I said: 'What's the matter?' She says: 'You look as if you've been dragged through a hedge backwards'. I said: 'I have'. Isn't that nice?

Two other stories, told to me by Simon Barrington-Ward, the retired Bishop of Coventry, give further insights into Roland Walls.

One day, Roland and I were walking together round 'the Backs' of the Colleges in Cambridge and ended up by walking through Trinity New Court (I think it's called), a Victorian part of the College opening onto the Backs. We were on our way back to Corpus Christi College, where Roland was then dean. In the corner of the court was a curious feature, a little pulpit looking down across the whole space. Roland looked at it whimsically and said: 'D'you know, it would be a wonderful thing if we could have for a year a complete moratorium on all Christian speaking, sermons, lectures, anything, a ban imposing total silence. I would then go and live up in the room behind that pulpit. And when the year's silence was over, the rumour would go round the whole of Cambridge: "The hermit will speak! The hermit will speak!" And a tremendous crowd would pour into this court until the whole place was full to overflowing. They would be packed together here and beyond! And suddenly I would appear in the pulpit, and, gazing out on the silent throng, I would call out solemnly, deeply, resonantly' – and then he said, very slowly with immense emphasis: '"Honesty ... is ... the ... best ... policy!" And a great sigh and groan would go up, "Oh! Oooooooh!", because the words would have recovered such meaning that everyone would be utterly staggered by their power!'

Simon's second tale further reveals how Roland Walls, for all his erudition as a theologian, was open to very direct and immediate epiphanies.

Roland told Jean and myself once, I think when we were all staying with Bishop Ken Carey, up at Kincraig, that at one time he was a strict Anglo-Catholic, perhaps more so than most products of Kelham, and would not have dreamt of receiving communion at a non-Episcopal church's communion service, although in many ways he was already obviously quite adventurously ecumenical. At that stage in his life, he went with a party to Iona and stayed there for a week, leading up to a splendid Sunday communion service. At this service, George MacLeod was presiding.

It happened that two large glass chalices had just arrived. George had commissioned them for the Iona Community from a Glasgow glazier. George had chosen a text to be inscribed on one of these chalices, I forget what, but it could well have been 'I am the Vine and you are the branches'. But George had decided that he would ask his friend the glazier, who happened to be agnostically if not atheistically inclined, to choose his own inscription from the New Testament to put on the other chalice. When the chalices, still in their box, were brought in and George unwrapped them, he read off the text the craftsman had chosen. It was 'Friend, wherefore art thou come?', the words of Jesus to Judas Iscariot in Gethsemane when he came up to Jesus and kissed him (Matthew 26:50 in the King James version). This created quite a sensation in the congregation.

When the bread and wine were passed along the rows, Roland saw the plate coming and behind it the chalice with that inscription. As it was handed along, the words kept appearing 'art thou come?' Suddenly Roland couldn't any longer stick to his principle of refusing the sacrament and passing it on. Then and there, he jettisoned the whole idea and took the bread and the wine! I quoted this once in a sermon in Westcott House in the week of prayer for Christian unity, and, unknown to me, an RC nun on the staff suddenly made the same decision! I would like to have been able to tell Roland that. He would have loved it!

The conversations in this book, taped over several years, provide periodic 'snapshots' of the steady yet ever-changing Community of the Transfiguration. By the time you read this, the configuration may have changed again. Above all, the conversations provide examples of the stimulating teaching of the Community's charismatic founder, who, when he was priest-in-charge at Rosslyn Chapel, was described by a bewildered but delighted member of his congregation as 'High as Rome, and low as the Kirk'.

At the time of writing, the Community of the Transfiguration is more fragile than it has ever been. Only Roland Walls, who is 88 years old and becoming quite frail, John Halsey, aged 71, and Patty Burgess, aged 89, remain. Roland has always known that it would be thus. Speaking of the origins of the Community, he said: 'I was realising that whatever I was going to do, it had to be precarious, it had to be fragile, not because it was the early stages of something that might grow into something big, but it had always of its nature to be fragile'.

John Halsey, Prior of the Community during its Bene-dictine association, and now Guardian Brother in its Franciscan incarnation, is a quiet hero in this story. He has been with Roland since the foundation of the community, and has stuck with it all the way through. Possessed of an acute theological mind, Brother John has been content to live somewhat in Roland's shadow. Without him, the community could not have functioned. He has been a rock. Patty Burgess, who for most of the time has lived – and still lives – at Loanhead, remains a committed source of joyous strength and wisdom.

It could well be that the Community of the Transfigura-tion will cease to exist in the comparatively near future. The huts and the house – battered places of prayer, hospitality, tears, craziness, forgiveness, laughter and inspiration – will inevitably decay, as well as the people, and will eventually remain only in the memory. This book is intended to keep that memory alive, just as my biography of Geoff Shaw was intended to keep alive the vision of the Gorbals Group. The Community of the Transfiguration and the Gorbals Group, both of which have consciously worked in an understated way, are two of the bravest and most inspiring experiments in gospel living in Britain in recent times.

Yet it is too simple to confine the Roslin venture to the realms of memory. Its essential life continues in the lives of the thousands of people who have made an alternative Roslin pilgrimage to that old miners' welfare institute and that silent enclosure with its five cells and a wooden chapel. The thirsty and sometimes life-wounded pilgrims have been seeking to drink industrial-strength real Christian ale, rather than to sip the frothy decaffeinated cappuccino of crazy conspiracy codes. Their holy grail has not been a physical treasure but a glimpse of one unusual – indeed eccentric, in the true meaning of that word – contemporary incarnation of the reality of the ancient and ever-renewing gospel of Christ.

This book attempts to be neither a full history of the Community of the Transfiguration nor a complete biography of Roland Walls. What it seeks to do is to convey their spirit to those who have never encountered it, and to encapsulate the unfolding significance of the place, so that others may be inspired and challenged. The conversational format of the book is appropriate to the man himself, who said: 'My job is to get people thinking, praying, talking, acting – *acting*! That's been my work. Through speech, really.'

Ron Ferguson

1

THE UPSIDE-DOWN
KINGDOM

Roland, how do you understand the kingdom of God?

One of the things that is really distressing about the switch
of attention from the phenomenal church to the kingdom
of God – which is good, and I'm wholeheartedly behind it
– is that, in making this tremendous shift from identifying
the kingdom of God with the church, most of us go to
town about *building* the kingdom. Now, so far as I know,
there is no mention in the Bible whatsoever of building
the kingdom, or indeed of building Jerusalem. *The Lord*
builds up Jerusalem, and he comes down from heaven to
us. And that deflected arrow from God to us is the constant
temptation of the zealous and the active.

*It's a common thing, isn't it, this talk of building the
kingdom, having a blueprint?*

That's right, as if we've got a blueprint, and all we've got
to do is build it. But that overthrows the essential good
news of the gospel, which is that it is all going to be *gift*.
It's going to *arrive*. You're going to *enter* it. You're going
to be *invited* to see it, to enter it, to be given it. And it's
going to arrive from God to us. Now, what do we mean
then by the kingdom of God? Is it here? Is it coming? What
are we actually offering people? Well, I think the kingdom

of God, in its meaning in the Aramaic and Greek, and in the Latin, *regnum*, means the *rule* of God: where God has his way, the kingdom comes. In the Lord's Prayer, we pray eschatologically about the end; but we also pray fervently: 'Thy will be done', *today*, by us – but also, in spite of us. Now, the kingdom comes when the will is done. So all we should do is either (a) make a space where God can himself do something, and we sit back and watch it, which is marvellous – most of the time God can't do any will of his because we're having our religious or spiritual wills fulfilled by ourselves – or (b) say: 'Well, look Lord, put me in the way of your will, so that I can do it by the insights and the strengths you've given me'. So in a way God's doing it, yes, through us. I believe that the kingdom can be prepared for by making a space, by following the little insignificant – seemingly insignificant – will of God, in how we spend money and how we treat one another and all the rest of it. But in the end the kingdom itself, the bliss of the kingdom, is sheer grace, nothing we can manage.

So the stuff about building the kingdom is a real heresy?

Yes, it's the usual Western semi-Pelagianism. When we ask anybody about the sacraments, when we talk about the Word, when we talk about prayer, theologically we *know* we have to avoid semi-Pelagianism – but in actual practice, especially in preaching, we get on to semi-Pelagianism, because it's so easy to invite people into some incredible *challenges* and all that nonsense. The word 'challenge' – another word that never appears in scripture – seems to occur until you're knee-deep in challenges after most sermons.

That's right, it's all about challenge, building and great exhortations ...

Yes! What are we going to *do* about it, and all that. The minister in the pulpit loves that bit of the sermon when he's done with all the exposition of the text and gets on to – well, what are we going to do about it?

That's one of the things that seems to run through the whole church spectrum – the challenge to build, produce some kind of results.

Those who preach that show the kind of 'oughtness' they're living with ...

There's a real anxiety there ...

... and a terrible guilt that they haven't done this or they haven't done that. That's what gives them the nerve to tell other people. And the terrible thing is that just at the moment when the Church of Rome is reviewing what it thinks of Luther – some of them going so far as to say that one of these days he'll be declared, in some of his writings, a Doctor of the Church – the Protestant world seems to have gone on to a works thing!

And doesn't the whole anxiety/works business tie up with success theology, which is a form of justification?

Yes. Unlike in the medieval church, the poor ministers today have to justify themselves. They've got to justify themselves to their people, to their bishop, to God – and to themselves! So they've got a fourfold justification programme working in their minds.

It's a horrific burden. For a tradition with justification by faith at its heart, it's a curious turn-around, isn't it?

It is *the* big paradox of church history. The primary ecumenical exercise, not only theological but pastoral and evangelical, is to return to the New Testament justification by faith – as long as it's interpreted not in the juridical form that Paul gave and led many of the Reformers into juridicism, but into the pure love-acceptance of the personalism of modern theology.

And life becomes a response to that, rather than building the kingdom.

It's so joyful you want all day to do it, it's marvellous! I believe the joylessness of a lot of what is happening comes from this oppression.

Because you can never win, can you? You can never meet the Lord's quotas.

The quota of the Lord is a pound, sixteen ounces, and all the most pious, zealous minister or layman can get is about twelve ounces.

It turns the gospel into bad news. It's upside-down, isn't it?

Therefore you've got this miserable thing of so-called 'failure'. 'Success' and 'failure' are judged in terms of this primary justification. You see, I believe that justification by works produces a success programme which is never completed, never going to be fulfilled, and in the end breaks the spirit of both layperson and minister.

And it gets tied up with numbers, doesn't it?

Yes. For example, here's one curious thing: when did they start this business of registering the numbers of people who attend services? When I was an Anglican, every time I celebrated the Eucharist I had to put in a book how many attended. I can't tell you the freedom that I have now. All I've got to do is to put my vestments on and go and say Mass. There's no book to sign or say it's happened or anything. Well, now, when did all that start, and does it go right through the denominations? Or is it something that is peculiar to Anglicanism? Because that book is important. The bishop looks at it when he comes, and church wardens are glad or sad about what the vicar puts down. Now, what's all that about?

The Church of Scotland publishes a Year Book *which is full of numbers. Every church has to give the numbers in the Woman's Guild and the Sunday School and so on. People reckon that that book should be on the shelves marked 'fiction'! Because of the success/competitive thing, ministers are sitting there saying: 'How many will I put into the Woman's Guild? I don't want to make it look too bad.' He's maybe got two old wifies and he puts down thirty or something – on a good day. And it's fiction.*

I heard a marvellous story which is not apocryphal, though it sounds it. One rector of an Episcopalian parish in Edinburgh in the 1930s was congratulated by his bishop publicly for the enormous rise in communicants all of a sudden in the parish. The man tried to interrupt the bishop in his praise, and the bishop put it down to humility. But then when he got a chance to speak, he said: 'My Lord, I must tell you, I made a mistake. I included *the year* in the numbers!' Isn't that marvellous? Well, now, it's this kind of little detail which really reveals the state of play. The oppression of *numbers* is a terrible thing because numbers in the gospel mean nothing at all, since we started off with one Christ and twelve men. The numbers aren't very significant, though I think Luke is a bit number-conscious. He tells us how many on the day of Pentecost were done and all that sort of thing. He's a little bit influenced by numbers – it shows that the little worm is coming in. The success of Pentecost is an idealised picture.

It then becomes another oppressive picture by which people measure themselves.

I believe that the Lucan account of Pentecost is a real bogey, because every priest and every minister would like a new Pentecost signified by thousands crowding out the doors, whereas the conversion of one man who became an Augustine or a Saint Basil in a congregation would pass unnoticed!

*So the way to depress yourself is to read the story of
Pentecost!*

Absolutely. I hear the most depressing sermons on the Feast
of Pentecost! [*Roland collapses in laughter.*]

An anxiety runs through the whole thing?

Yes. There's me with a busted balloon in my hand – and
there's this huge great balloon going up with this hot
air, that's the great Spirit's arrival! Now, I believe that
that's done untold damage – the way we've interpreted it
– perhaps even because of Luke's influence, I don't know.

*So, Roland, what should a minister or a priest who
sees through this theology of success and the oppressive
numbers game that goes with it be doing?*

Well now, you see, beside the number thing, I think there's
another business which I've noticed at clerical meetings.
When they get out their books for the date of the next
meeting, you're not supposed to be free on the first day
mentioned – that's part of the game. You say: 'Oh, I
couldn't manage that date'. That's the first thing. The
second thing is, the more you show that you can't manage
for, say, five dates in a row, people look up and think:
'Look at me, I've got blank pages'. Now, the man who
is doing well in engagements lets his diary be seen. Very
often, he will put it in such a way that his neighbours at
least can see this crowded page. The poor man who seems
to be doing nothing hides the fact that he's got weeks and
weeks without anything going on at all. So there's another
preoccupation: busyness. Preoccupation with numbers and
busyness is always a symptom of the disease.

'Success' in the Christian enterprise has to pass through
this lonely man, Jesus, who failed completely. Mr Moonie
has based a whole religion on the failure of Jesus Christ. So,
somehow or other, theologically, and therefore spiritually,
the success addict's disease is that he's left the centre,

because the centre isn't very encouraging. And therefore it has something to do with what does he think about Christ, and whose son is he, and how far did *he* get? You can always keep the success story going with a resurrection – but the resurrection of Christ isn't the flip-over of the coin, it's showing the *value* of the coin.

The resurrection doesn't cancel the crucifixion out.

No, it's the crucified who is risen and therefore got the approval of God. So we've got to beware lest we come back with an easy theology of resurrection to justify success.

That's right. And you get the positive-thinking success story for individuals. When I was in North Carolina, I heard a radio preacher saying: 'If you believe in Jesus, get ready to move house – you're going to move to a bigger house'. He was a very popular preacher. He was using the text about making mountains move as a justification for saying that you'll move up in the world, if you believe.

That is fantastic, because that is the very reversal of what Christ was saying! Christ was saying: 'If you believe, be prepared to lose the lot!' Now, how can such a reversal happen in history at all? It's a phenomenon which needs a great deal of examination, because although we're not as crude as some of the American evangelists, we say 'Why me?' when disaster falls. 'Look at me, I've done all I can, yet the Lord's removed everything from me, including my health.' Even lurking in the mind of the person trying to think it through, he still has the expectation that in order to get this marvellous gospel right, he's got to be given health and strength and money and status and power.

It is an amazing reversal.

It's extraordinary, because there's no way in which you could justify it from the givenness of the revelation. It's just the very opposite. How did it happen? I think it's a left-over – which has got a virulent sort of lifespan still – from Constantinian religion. It goes back to the time when the Empire first approved of us, and the Pope was given the letter and the palace to live in – instead of the little tenement 'semi' that he had in the suburbs of Rome. In fact, Sylvester the First was canonised because he made the move. He lived in quite a different apartment from Miltiades, his predecessor, who lived in a sort of but-and-ben somewhere. From then on, the church did have affluence and riches and goodness knows what. It built itself up. It looked as if God had blessed us all at last with the wherewithal to spread the kingdom, and so you got this grand, majestic state of Constantinian Christianity, whose last days we are seeing, and at whose burial we hope to preside.

It's almost like a temptation of Christ. Being shown the kingdoms. It's as if we've swallowed that one – hook, line and sinker.

I think they did ascend a mountain of majesty and see the devil's kingdom. When they said 'You could have it', they took it – with great intentions to do the will of God through it. The church of Christ fell, whereas Christ stood. Now, there was always the thin red line, of course, of the people who knew that that was not the way. Thank God there is a whole history of saints who knew the score and kept it going one way and another. It made the monk very relevant to the preaching of the gospel, by his life. So it wasn't all lost, but I think this success stuff really goes back to that.

And this fundamental flaw in the whole thing leads straight through to the modern ministers being oppressed by the demand for statistics.

That's right. You've got to think of it as being historically explainable somehow, because otherwise it would be a phenomenon which would be so mysterious, wouldn't it?

It also explains why the minister reads explosive stuff from the Bible and no-one reacts. There's been a thousand years of conditioning.

Yes, historically we got that magnificent, imperial, global approval, and we now expect approval from everybody – from society, from our congregation, from our bishop. We want approval, and the mark of approval is everybody saying: 'You're doing well', which means numbers, and busyness. But it's extraordinary how Constantine's bound up with the success of American evangelism today.

It's a whole line, isn't it? Straight down – and it's a complete heresy.

Now, you see, at the Feast of the Conversion of Blessed Paul this year, I had to preach a little homily at Mass and it dawned on me then that church history is really the slow but inevitable breaking through – against all comers – of certain basic truths that couldn't have been obvious at the beginning. For example, take the whole business of the opening of the door to the Gentiles, which was the great crisis of all times. It meant that the Christian Church didn't remain a Jewish sect. The church would have disappeared if Paul and Peter hadn't told of their experiences and got it through the Council of Jerusalem, which was the most important of all the councils. With the option for the poor, we are witnessing an enormous second great movement. It's of tremendous consequence, however much it is filled with rhetoric and hasn't been followed up.

Just as the Gentile one wasn't followed up by all the churches at the time, so, in the same way, we're not all taking on the rhetoric or the declaration of the Church today. But the option for the poor is the great second breakthrough to humanity. It wasn't on the plate when I was a Christian in my youth. It's a geological shift in the church's foundation, and it's of enormous consequence. They will date the twentieth century in time to come as one of the most important centuries of the church's history. And therefore when we get despairing, when we have our nose to the grindstone and all we can see is what's round us for a few miles, the great way of being joyful is to lift up our heads and see what is happening in some enormous millennial perspective, as God sees it.

Roland, what do you think of the use of the word 'crusade' by evangelists?

Paradoxically, an unacceptable word has become acceptable. Just at the time when we are all of us confessing what a nonsense the Crusades were, we are using it in this other sense. Again, it's all about success. The Crusades are now seen as one of the most hopeless, stupid blunders of Christian history. The word seems to be still lively in some quarters; we still talk about an evangelical 'crusade' – and without the word 'crux' (cross) being operative in it. A crusade is about an advance of a highly powerful lot of people getting a conquest. I find it strange and a bit alarming that certain sections of the British Christian scene can go on using a word which in the history books has gone down the drain in my lifetime. When I learned history, the Crusades weren't something you apologised for. They were seen rather as a necessity. And it was regarded as unfortunate that the third and fourth Crusades didn't come off as well as expected. The history books didn't apologise for the Crusades, but nowadays it's a burden on the Christian conscience. And yet the word seems to perpetuate itself without any attention to the word 'cross' in it. That seems to me to be very odd.

It uses all the very modern technology, and again it becomes very statistical. Reports of revivals are mostly statistical. The whole notion of a crusade is very strange. You can't imagine Jesus mounting a crusade. You can't imagine Jesus saying to the disciples: 'We're moving on to Jerusalem for the crusade – would you get the posters up?'

It would be like a lot of clowns doing it! It would be like a charade, wouldn't it? We're always embarrassed over what to do about Palm Sunday celebrations because you've got to be kids doing a charade on Palm Sunday when the church gives out palm leaves and they have a little procession and it's cracked voices singing: 'All glory, laud and honour', with kids dressed up in a tablecloth doing a little nonsense! And the Lord knew it, and he loved it, because that's as far as we can ever get with any kind of show.

Now, the funny thing is that when it comes to numbers, the gospel-writers tell us about 5,000 or 4,000, not the numbers who came to *hear* him, but the numbers he *fed*. That's a different thing. Now, if we could get new church statistics, they ought to be about the numbers we've really *given to*, unconditionally – like the feeding of the crowd. It was unconditional. It was an abundance of grace. It wasn't about how many people were won for the Lord. How we twist all this! With that gospel story, we can all of us think: 'What a marvellous success story – he got 5,000 to listen to him!' But that wasn't the point of the gospel story. It was how many were *fed*. Now, if we want statistics, that's the way they ought to be presented: how many have you touched – rather than 'got in'.

Even the disciples were into this success stuff too, weren't they – arguing about who was going to be first in the kingdom, when Jesus was actually heading for Jerusalem.

Success was written into what they wanted. And Peter's thing – 'Far be it from you, Lord!' That wasn't the way he wanted him to go. So it's endemic in the discipleship thing from the start.

It's almost a response to anxiety – again about justifying. These guys had to justify having left home.

Yes, they even said: 'What are we going to have for it?' They actually asked the question! He said: 'You'll get a lot of friends ... plus the executions!'

'How many converts did you make in Jerusalem, Jesus?'
'Actually, I was crucified.' He was a big failure, wasn't he?

He was the biggest failure in the world. Old Moonie's right to base his religion on the failure of Jesus Christ.

The Jerusalem crusade failed on all fronts. It ended up with the prime guy being killed!

It's a magnificent sequence, because it all happened within a week. On Monday, the *Jerusalem Post* reported about a lot of kids who came to the temple and sang hymns, and the clergymen didn't like all this much. But soon the news changed. The very next day again, it looks like a success story. This wealthy woman comes and buys all this ointment and pours it out on Christ's feet. Then he says: 'She's anointed me for burial'. That was a *fantastic* statement.

It must have caused a wee hush in the conversation, all that talk about burial. The guys are working on their crusade material, and Jesus starts talking about burial!

They're worrying about their follow-up programme for the converts.

They're getting their counsellors ready ...

Don't you think it's heaven? It's wonderful! Even in the celebration of Holy Week you can pietise Palm Sunday, you can pietise the whole blooming thing. It's terrifying what you can do!

It's almost a 'must' to make Holy Week into a success story. You can say: 'We had fifty on Monday night', and so on.

It's a great time when you can really check up on one another. At the deanery meetings, you hear them saying: 'Maundy Thursday Mass – oh, it was absolutely crowded'.

'Oh, so was ours! In fact, we had to relay the Mass into the hall.' Any advance on that? Then the Easter vigil, good life! 'Do you know that at the Easter vigil it took twenty minutes to give communion to everybody!' It's terrible stuff, you know. I never cease wondering at the whole turn-around!

The more you look at it, the more staggering it is, because there is nothing in the gospels which would tend to this conclusion at all.

Not at all. In fact, the very reverse. The whole thing's about a different story. So, when people talk about evangelism, we've really got to ask: 'Well, what gospel are you going to proclaim?' It's as simple as that. One of the marvellous things is that the Lord prevents ordinary blokes from coming in because it's all been turned upside down. Inarticulate and unconscious, they know that it's not what the clergy say it is, so they're not going to come.

It's about truth, isn't it?

About truth, and authenticity. Unless the authenticity of the living, preached and expectant gospel stuff is there, the ordinary bloke – he's given this marvellous gift of common sense – won't be there. He can smell truth, even under his sins and his apathy, and all that. He may not follow it, but at least he knows when it's truth and not a lot of guff. Why go along? What would be the point of getting up to a huge dressed-up human activity when the *raison d'être* of it has disappeared under the heap of so-called 'celebration'? I mean, they *know* ... thank God.

It's almost like a form of hypnosis, in which we don't notice the contradiction at the heart of it all.

It's like we're in a dream, almost as if we're zombie-like. Partly because there's been a kind of crypto-programming which affects our catechesis from Sunday School days,

Christ has been made into a success story. We hear that very often, from a very early age.

Christianity becomes a 'world religion', and you cover parts of the globe with colours.

When I went to Glasgow for a marvellous interfaith gathering, to my horror I saw somebody had got out some Sunday School map of world religions. The whole of North America and South America were coloured purple, the whole of Europe to the Urals was coloured purple. There was a great growing streak of blue ink covering East Africa and the Arab countries. Red was the colour for Hindus and of course yellow for the Buddhists. Now what was the object of the exercise with that map? Did they think that the purple ink that had been rather generously scattered over the USA was going to cover all the rest? Or the blue? What was the purpose of the exercise? It was imperial! It's just like those maps of the British Empire – to impress. The purple was bigger than any of the rest!

The 'success' orientation turns Christianity into an ideology, doesn't it? A crusading ideology at that.

As soon as you move away from the person of Christ, as soon as you move away from that divine humanity, you're sunk in every direction. This whole business is not really about a theological perception of the church, it's about fidelity to a person. And all of this, whether about the Gentiles, or options for the poor or whatever the next move is, is really about Jesus. If it isn't about that, it's either some theological paradigm or ideology, political or religious, and it creates division. Each move is either getting into the catholicity of Jesus or it's moving into the sectarian force of religion. And the big problem for the twenty-first century is going to be the divisive force of religion and nationalism. That's our next stop. Religion has really got to look at this one. We've got a very bad press at present. We're now included with racism, class and nationalism. The *Guardian* newspaper is always totting up all the divisive things in humanity – and, quite rightly, from their point of view, religion features in the list. If the gospel can't get itself out of religion, in the sense of this imperial, triumphal, divisive stuff, then it's not going to be faithfully preached and proclaimed. If anybody asked me what is the purpose of my life as I see it now, I would say it's to contribute, in however small a way, to getting the gospel seen as transcendent to human religion.

There was an interesting television programme called
Guns and Rosaries *recently. It was about clergy in New York, in Brooklyn, in all the drugs scene. Some of the congregation were carrying guns to protect themselves. They interviewed one priest who was shocked, saying: 'We can't have any truck with this business of carrying guns'. Other ministers and priests said that the drugs scene was such that they needed to carry guns.*

This is where you get the crunch point of self-preservation. What would one do oneself? If we lived in a society which was crazed with crack, we'd have to face this. Now, here we get again the question: 'What are you prepared to die for?'

The woman who was interviewing this minister said: 'But isn't this contrary to the Christian message?' He replied: 'Christ commands me to love you, but not to die for you'.

He said that?

Yes. And he said: 'If a man comes in with a gun, I shoot him'. It's interesting how you get these reversals. It's turning the whole thing on its head.

One hundred and eighty degrees, right round.

He said it without any ambiguity. It was really quite astonishing. The whole situation there was a complete mess. People running around with guns were robbing ministers and rabbis and nuns for money for crack, and some of the clergy were saying that guns are the only answer.

You see, theology is like a chameleon. It can actually justify. You use your rational attitude to work out a justification for action which is humanly sane, but Christianly impossible.

One of the clerics who was interviewed took the argument about violence back to Constantine. He said that in terms of the private Christian individual, what was happening in New York was a kind of private 'just war' – and therefore you were entitled to defend yourself, and that there were occasions when it was right to use violence. Some clerics argued that it was the lesser of two evils to carry some kind of deterrent and even to kill.

Doesn't this illustrate the fact that Constantinian stuff is over? But the real movement is away from this power and protection and stuff, citadel stuff, out into the rather vulnerable and martyrdom business, which is really about getting hold of the faith commitment side of Christian adherence. It seems to me we're in a kind of halfway house whereby we're having to live all the time with Constantinian assumptions, and stand up from time to time. But we don't know what we're going to do until something happens. We don't know how much hold this has got on us. You can't just do it intellectually.

On the TV programme, they interviewed one of the prosecutors in New York, who's handled a lot of murder cases. The woman said to him: 'What about this business of clergy carrying guns?' He said: 'If the clergy start carrying guns, what does that say? It seems to me to be a complete contradiction.' This guy was not a churchman, and he was able to see it very clearly.

As soon as you believe, and you take Christ on board, the real, basic question is 'What are you prepared to die for?' This is really important. And we haven't any answer in our comfortable, cosy existence, until something drastic happens. But that particular question raises the whole issue of how far a Constantinian-based Christianity is going to get through in the future. I don't think it has any chance of getting through ...

No, it's no longer up to the job, is it, given the realities of the situation? The minister in his dark suit and dog collar, sitting there and saying: 'I'm called to love you, not to die for you', contradicts the theological talk about a loving, dying God. Yet you can appreciate the man's dilemma. You don't know how you would react yourself. But you do know that there's something really seriously wrong here.

Yes, for someone who is not just a follower, but a minister and a teacher, to state something which is so categorically against everything we've been taught by Christ. You've got to get to what is the one thing that matters. What is the one thing necessary? I find myself tussling with this problem all the time, because I believe it's answering this that is going to be our real service to the human race. It really is going to be about helping the human race to find its unity round the centre which is *real* and *there*, rather than some imaginary utopian liberal dream, or what we can get through education, or whatever it is. We must answer the *despair* of the human race, not its hopes. The new generation is fed up to the teeth with dreams.

The twentieth century's dreams – utopianism, Nazism and communism – were all causes of fear and destruction.

All these gods with clay feet have come down, in our own lifetime. We daren't go back to looking as if we've got another one. You know, we've got only a little stone from the mountain, Christ, from the mountain of God – a little stone that has broken the idols. I think that's a tremendous thing.

Isn't it true that Christianity as an ideology has failed, just as much as Marxism?

Absolutely, and we've got to be fearlessly saying: 'We have, in history, misled generations'. And we've got to be able to say that without false humility, just facing reality about ourselves and about our own traditions.

When we think about Germany and the Holocaust, we can see that the German nation was no stranger to Christian teaching. And that's not simply to blame Germany. The capacity for that is universal.

It's the capacity of all of us. That's the awful thing about the Holocaust. It's not as if we can make a scapegoat out of it. There's no scapegoat except ourselves. That's why, going back to this centre of relational love, the whole business of forgiveness, as a human activity, is essential to our self-understanding. Otherwise we can either project guilt on somebody else, or take it upon ourselves with no release, which ends in paralysis of action and being.

When we were in Easterhouse, in Glasgow, I remember my daughter running home from school. We asked her: 'What have you been doing?' She said: 'The Kafflix (Catholics) were chasing us'. And, of course, she was a 'Prodisant' (Protestant). These were names of tribes. And so it ends up in football clubs, and it's got nothing to do with anything. It's got something to do with Christianity as an ideology, and a crusading success story.

Yes, there's a Protestant formula and a Catholic formula. It's absolutely endemic to Scottish religion. I remember meeting John Habgood, the Archbishop of York. He said: 'Roland, I've discovered something I never knew before. The basis of the establishment in Scotland is quite a different thing from the establishment in England.' I said: 'Well, I know the constitution is different, but what's so marvellous about that?' 'No,' he said, 'not only that. I've just been to Scotland, and I find that the Church of Scotland is worried because the Roman Catholics look as if they're going to be equal, and then surpass the Kirk – then, of course, it wouldn't be the religion of the nation any more, and Scotland's establishment stuff would suffer a hammering. Whereas in the Church of England, so long as me and Canterbury and the Queen belong to the C of E, the establishment would stand! Everywhere I went I heard a kind of anxiety – an anxiety which doesn't stem from any kind of thought about it, it's just a matter of numbers. It made me realise the kind of establishment line we're upholding. We can get on with three people. I think it would be a bit of a crisis if one of the Archbishops or the Queen herself stopped being an Anglican, but otherwise we're here forever.'

All this came out because I had asked him: 'John, are you still banging this establishment drum?' 'Oh yes,' he said, 'for good theological reasons.' So I said: 'It's a dead horse. We're the only nation left, except for Sweden or something, where we have got all this nonsense. I mean, it's gone, it's dead. You've got about two inches left, and then you'll hit bare rock if you haven't already.'

2

THE MAKING OF AN ANGLICAN CAMBRIDGE DON

Roland, could you tell me about the dates and circumstances of your birth and your upbringing?

Right. Well, I was born at Bembridge, Isle of Wight, at half past three in the afternoon of the 7th June 1917. That happened to be – though I don't think my parents knew it, and I didn't know it until I was about twelve years old – Corpus Christi day.

When you were very young, who do you think nurtured your faith?

My mother. My father wasn't particularly enamoured of the faith, I think. He wasn't an unbeliever, but he wasn't like my mother, he didn't have an almost natural gratitude to God or anything like that. And he wasn't involved, I don't think, at all, in my early religious upbringing.

My mother was an extremely humble woman. Not that she would know it, of course; but she had married a very domineering man who liked his own way, and I soon picked that up. One thing I discovered was that there was a different sort of power about in the family, which came – well, I don't know if it was power, but a kind of mesh, an energy – coming from a woman who was always a bit of a doormat. It wasn't just mere acquiescence, it was a positive thing, which I noticed. Very early on, I think I picked that up. And this has conditioned my impatience with my own self-will, which I get from my father, and will predominate, which I have got to watch.

So the example of your mother perhaps led you on to reflections about power in your later life?

Yes. Well, when I did theology, I picked up one or two things which I knew on my pulse, which I found confirmed in what I knew about theology and the humanity of Christ. I think that we had a one-to-one understanding which helped me considerably then. But of course, she didn't influence me in the sense that I naturally, or even supernaturally, acquired this virtue. All my life, I've had to struggle against this other thing, of wanting my own way and wanting to be top dog and all that.

But nevertheless, observing your mother and the power which came from powerlessness, in your mother ...

... Yes. That's it. That was early on.

And that has undoubtedly led you to be here in this place, where powerlessness becomes a focus.

Yes, it's really my Mum all over again. This time, myself making what I hope to be a safe framework where my natural propensities might have a chance of being trained.

Did your mother do for you the things which a Christian upbringing normally requires, such as catechism and confirmation?

Yes, She was a devout – she wasn't sophisticated – very simple woman, this daughter of an illiterate father and a school-teaching mother. My grandfather was illiterate, and had to have the gospel read to him by his pious wife, who was my grandmother. And this natural piety expressed itself in a kind of very pedestrian Anglicanism, which wasn't party, didn't think in terms of whether anybody was different, they just went on with what they found at the parish church, which was sort of middle-to-off evangelical. But she had a bit of a horror of Anglo-Catholicism, and Rome would be outside her reach. I mean, she would talk about people: 'She's a Catholic but she's very nice'. That kind of thing, in a natural, British sort of way! But she had no sophistication about it. She had a natural piety which was absolutely founded on gratitude.

And these were Isle of Wight folk?

Yes, in Bembridge. And the poverty, which she experienced and we all experienced in the 1930s, was because my father was unemployed for five years during that period from mid-1929 to 1934. Just in my last years of school, I became politically aware through the poverty of an unemployed person living on – whatever it was – thirty bob a week.

When you say 'politically aware', what form of politics did that take?

Oh, it was radical from the beginning. Because I realised that my mother, my dear mother, scrubbed the steps of the rich in cold winter weather, with hands blue with cold and rough from the soda in those days. And I noticed all this; and I noticed the rich, who went out all day, and came home to a great four-course dinner that was prepared by my aunt – not my real aunt, but my mother's friend Nelly – who was the cook in the same household that my mother did for. I noticed all this, and I thought, what an extraordinary arrangement! I also noticed the rather condescending generosity of these people who would hand me down a suit that one of their sons who was at Eton or some public school grew out of, and I got – with great pleasure, but all the same I noticed all this very early on.

And what was your programme for changing all this?

I didn't have a programme; I had a kind of subdued and subconscious anger about it, more an uneasiness. I had a kind of anger about how my mother was having to do all this for a pittance. Because this was all the money we were earning.

Where were you educated?

I was educated at a Board school in Bettesworth Road primary and then St John's Road Upper Grade school – these names, of course, 'Upper Grade', are gone long – in Ryde, Isle of Wight, and then I went at the age of I suppose 11 or 12, to Sandown grammar school, where I remained until 1934.

How come you were led from this background to Kelham, with its quite Anglo-Catholic ways?

Well, first of all I learnt my Anglo-Catholic ways by being extremely naughty when I was a boy. I was out for a walk with my Auntie Gertie, my mother's sister, and we were passing St Michael and All Angels, a fantastically high church in Swanborne, a suburb of Ryde. I'd been going – because there was no decent ordinary religion going on up there – to a kind of Congregationalist chapel place, *faute de mieux* for Mum. She'd rather I went to the Anglican church, but there wasn't anything that was trustworthy. I hadn't really noticed this church to ask about it, until I was about six or seven, and I said to my Auntie Gertie: 'What's that place?' She says: 'That's a church, dear'. 'Why don't we go to that church?' 'You mustn't go in there, because they worship the Virgin Mary in there', said my Auntie Gertie. I pricked up my ears; I thought, how interesting. That's something rather more exciting than this rather boring God that everybody seems to have a go at! So I thought, the next Sunday, instead of

going to the little chapel place for Sunday School at three
o'clock, I would go in with somebody I knew who went
to St Michael and All Angels. I was overjoyed to find that
they didn't meet in a ghastly hall with radiators and a
Chief Scout and all that sort of thing, but they met in the
church, which was fantastic – six great candlesticks at the
tabernacle, I didn't understand any of it at all, and in the
corner, to my delight, I saw a life-size statue of the Mother
of God. And I thought, oh my goodness, we're going to do
something about that!

You didn't know who she was?

Yes, I knew she was Mary; because we read the gospel;
we had a family Bible and we were read to by Mum on
Sundays and all that. Oh yes, we were brought up to
know the Bible. As Newman says, the British religion
is the Bible, and he's absolutely right. Well now, to my
great disappointment, this Sunday School went on in
rather the same way – though of course within a different
setting – as the Sunday School up there. They had Bible
stories, somebody told you all about it, and I thought,
well I wish they'd get on with the real business which is to
do something about her in the corner, you see! Well, we
didn't do anything about her at all! We all went out and I
thought, Oh, that's pretty dull! But never mind, there must
be something in it. She's there, anyway. So I persisted. To
my horror, one Thursday afternoon, my mother told me
when I got back from school that the vicar had called
and said how delighted he was that I was attending the
Sunday School – which she didn't know about – and that
he'd come to ask her permission to make me an altar boy!
[*Wheezes with laughter.*] I don't think I got a tanning that
night when Father came home, but I really was very set
back into wondering whether there was any freedom of
religion in the country! However, slowly, by my whining
and complaining, I was allowed to take up again the

position in the Sunday School, and got as far as being a choirboy, but not an altar boy. So I knew something about it. And I also knew, very early on, when I met all that, that I wanted to be a priest.

When you say 'very early on', what particular age occurs to you?

Well, even before that – this God stuff really haunted me, for two reasons. One: after the First World War, my father was away with the army in India and there was a lot of clearing-up stuff on the frontier provinces. Father didn't see me until I was about four years old. And I had been put out, while Mother was working to keep everything going, to live with an old Methodist couple who were really very formative for me. They were highly devout Methodists – rather narrow, but extremely committed. And I used to hear them, when I went to bed – over my bed was a lovely picture of the infant Samuel kneeling by his bed listening to the voice of God. I used to hear these two old people praying to God out loud, and reading the scriptures to one another, and this impressed me no end. Every night for about an hour, enormous prayer, a prayer meeting between the two of them.

And the death of my only sister, I think, again, was a strand of my vocation. Somehow or other, the effect of this death on me – she was only nine months old when she died – was to transfer, in a Newman kind of way, my interest into what was beyond death, and find it more important than what was going on around me. To a small child – I mean this was when I was about six – I can remember then knowing that I could pray to her. This was very strange. I could pray to my sister. I don't think I ever prayed *for* her. But I remember praying *to* her. Because she was somewhere where things that were important took place! And because of that, I thought – I didn't think, this wasn't choate thought – but I really ...

... It was more instinctive.

Instinctively, I knew that my job was to do with all that. And nothing really interested me about ordinary jobs that you do on earth. And it was in this extraordinary reaction to the death of my sister, who was intensely alive for me, and was in a far more interesting dimension than I was by being in all this stuff.

By the way, the other factor in my vocation to the priesthood was seeing this marvellous parish priest, Father Durham, who was the vicar of St Michael's at that time, when I was about 10 or 11 I suppose, when I was on my way home from school on a very snowy day. I saw him ploughing around in the snow from house to house, and this moved me. I'd seen him before going around, he was a very good pastor, he was one of the sights, just accepted, going round every afternoon week in week out, doing his visits – but when I saw him ploughing about in the snow, something touched me, and I thought that if that good man can spend his life doing that, I wouldn't mind a go.

My father, as I said, was unemployed, and to his great delight he discovered a job in a marvellous hamlet called St Lawrence, about three miles from Ventnor, on the Undercliff of the Isle of Wight, a delightful spot. He got a job at a hotel, as a kitchen porter plus waiter. The hotel was run by two appalling women who really gave hell to my father, and we couldn't understand why he'd ever said yes to it, but of course you had to say yes to anyone. He was lucky to get a job after five years. We moved into what we thought, as kids, was marvellous. It was a house over a stable, and it was only just about 200 yards from the sea. The nearest church of my variety, which I now had got used to, was St Alban's Ventnor, which was on our side of Ventnor. So we used to walk three miles to this church. When we got there, there was this marvellous priest called Fr Bernard Haraldsey, a young priest with his first parish, a magnificent person, who's had a tremendous effect on my life. After I told my father, at the age of 14, that I wanted to be a priest, he said: 'Oh well, you can put that out of your mind, sonny, we haven't got a bean', and in those days you had to go to university on your own money, unless you got a state scholarship. There was one for each county, and the chance of getting one was nil; and then you went to a theological college, but you had to pay your way. Without money, you couldn't be a priest in the Church of England.

So Fr Haraldsey –

He asked me: 'What are you going to do when you grow up?', and I said: 'Father, I want to be a priest'. 'Oh,' he says, 'that's marvellous!' And for the first time – except for one master at my school, who was a devout evangelical Christian – here was a priest saying yes to me! So I said: 'Yes, but my father says I must put that out of my mind, because we've got no money, it's ridiculous, impossible'. He says: 'Well, it's pretty hard, but there's one place that'll take you, and if they think you've got a vocation, they'll train you for nothing!' I thought: 'Cor!' He says: 'Don't build your hopes up, there's quite a long list. D'you want me to write?' I said yes. So he wrote off to the Society of the Sacred Mission. I went on July 6th – every day, it's imprinted on my mind – July 6th, the Octave of Saint Peter and Paul. I went to this place for a weekend to see them. It is near Newark-on-Trent, and was then the headquarters of the Society of the Sacred Mission. I was amazed to go north of London. We'd only been twice to London; by the age of 14, I hadn't been north of London, nor did I think anybody lived there really. To get on a train at King's Cross, and to be travelling north so far, and for so many hours, and still finding houses, was to me a wonder!

That was the first miracle that I registered in my life. By 'miracle' I mean an invasion from outside, to put something right that was impossible. By this time I was 17, when I'd just done my sixth-form stuff.

I was amazed at this monastery I went to. And oh, the yearning to be there, yet knowing that it was a one-to-100 chance of getting in! We'd moved back to Ryde into the most appalling squalid flat, the only place we could get, having given up everything in Ryde and gone to this hotel. My father in the end couldn't take any more, nor could they, and so we were back in Ryde. There was bacon fat over my bed where there had been a gas stove, and poor Mother used to cry because we had no money to put it right; the whole wall was dripping with bacon fat, which you just scraped off but it was still there – the whole thing was incredible – at a time when we had to sell the piano, the only thing of any value in the house, because we didn't have any money, and my poor mother was really broken-hearted over that. Now, a month later, I received a letter in the post with instructions to come in September to start studies at the junior bit of the seminary. I cried – I cried for hours by my bedside that night, in giving thanks to God for getting me into that. I couldn't believe it. I read, over and over again, the instructions, the little photographs, the brochure they sent about it all, and all the things I had to take. I was nonplussed, because even the few things that I had to take, I didn't have – things like dressing gown, pyjamas, slippers. Things like that which we'd never had. And I thought, well, the Lord will provide, and so he did. Auntie Nellie, this friend of my mother's, coughed up; and she coughed up, too, for my fare back to Ryde for the holidays. We were so poor, we couldn't even get my fare back to Ryde! Now, this poverty stuff not only started me off politically, but is and was and always has to be, it seems to me, a marvellous school for the gospel. It is beyond anything, when your limitations of choice and possessions are so great that you have to pray them down! Literally. And so it happened.

So the miracle happened, of your going to Kelham against all the odds. And you were aged 17 when you got there.

Yes. I went into this junior seminary for twenty-five, thirty nippers, who did a year or two years' pre-theological training in philosophy, history and languages. I stayed at Kelham, trained by the Society of the Sacred Mission, for six years.

At Kelham, what sort of theological tradition was in the ascendant at that time?

At that time, the founder of the society, Father Herbert Kelly, was still teaching, and I would say he was certainly not categorisable by the usual Anglo-Catholic, Liberal, Evangelical bits of the Church of England. He was a Barthian before Barth. In fact, when I was teaching theology later on and had to read the twelve volumes of Barth, most of it was familiar to me through the teaching of Father Kelly. He himself was a strange maverick, who very few people understood. William Temple was one of the few people who understood him, and Kelly always said that the other person who understood him was the little girl who typed out his books. But Kelly was strange, and he was an educator by provocation and perversity which is quite a useful stock in trade – tools of a good educator.

After your six years at Kelham, you had done your training. What happened after that?

I was ordained in December of 1940 to the diaconate, to a title at St James' Manston, which is a suburb of Leeds. I stayed there two and a half years and then I went back, at the request of the Kelham Fathers, to work in a parish which they ran in Sheffield. So in 1943 I removed myself to St Cecilia's, Parson Cross, a parish of 40,000 worked by a staff of seven Kelham priests, with three churches. I remained there until 1945.

It's customary nowadays to expect, sometimes even to encourage, young people to go through a period of doubt and wandering. Did this ever happen to you?

No, not then.

Later?

Yes. Oh, *very* much so. This was when the next miracle occurred. The next miracle was given to me on a plate, when I didn't need it and I shouldn't have asked for it. And it was probably absolutely against what I would now tell people to pray about. I was once making, when I was a young curate in Leeds, a retreat at the monastery of the community of St John the Evangelist, in Cowley, Oxford. And one day during the retreat, on a lovely October afternoon I think it was – lovely mellow sunlight on the lovely honey-coloured walls of the Colleges – I passed Magdalene. It must have been about five o'clock in the evening. I looked through one of the windows abutting the street, and there was a student in his room, with a little table-lamp, his books open on his little desk, and I prayed to God. I said: 'Lord, if it's your will, I would love to go to a university – which, of course, I can't'. Well, in those days, Kelham men were thought to be rather sort of not quite part of the old-boy network of the established church, and I knew that. I'd registered that fact, politically and ecclesiastically, and it has something to do with my later conversion to Rome.

Powerlessness again?

Mmm. But also, a kind of revulsion against this. I had this double thing, okaying it and saying yes, that's where I want to be, in spite of these blighters, but nevertheless not being content to see the blighters flourish! So there was a political and a gospel thing going on all the time, you see! And rather pulling me apart. This has always been so, I think. Do you do this, or do you say: Thank God I've got nothing!

Or that somebody else has got nothing? Do you have to do anything? So the politics and the gospel blessing of poverty has always been having a bit of warfare in my mind. Still does. Still does. But at that time, I asked for this prayer. Blow me. It's unbelievable. In my next move from my first parish, I went to work with the Kelham Fathers to help pay them back, out of gratitude; they wanted somebody to help them with a parish team in Sheffield, and I said yes, much against my spiritual adviser's advice, and against the parish priest I was working for, but I felt I owed – any request from them came to me as a kind of repayment, so I went. I did three years of that. At the end of those three years, the director of the Society of the Sacred Mission came to Sheffield and said: 'I want you to stop parish work and get prepared for theological teaching'. I thought that meant going back to Kelham, and he says: 'We plan to send you to Cambridge, and we would like you to try and get entrance into Corpus Christi College'. I did. I did a theological degree and was elected to a fellowship. I was an undergraduate from 1945 to 1948 at Corpus Christi College, Cambridge. As a result of the degree, in 1948 I was elected to a fellowship at the college – but a non-residentiary fellowship, because I felt I owed it to the Society to teach at their college at Kelham. So I was straddled between Cambridge, to which I returned for governing body meetings and various functions of the college there, and teaching in a monastic seminary where I taught New Testament until 1951.

During that time I'd become a novice, because I was so associated with the Society that I thought I ought to test my vocation with them. But in 1951 it became clear to me and to my advisers outside the Society that that particular vocation wasn't mine. So I left the novitiate, and I thought at that time it was right that I should also leave the seminary, because the seminary and the Society were very close together. I found myself not only with a non-residentiary fellowship, but they gave me a fellowship as Chaplain and Dean of the College. I was there for ten years. So I got this, but it wasn't a very good reason. It was rather a selfish little reason – that I saw that undergraduate in Magdalene and I wanted to be there.

As I had a year to spare before I could take up my fellowship as a residentiary at Cambridge, I became, rather absurdly, the chaplain to the Bishop of Ely for a year. It must have been the most absurd year for him and for me, because I had no gifts that would make me a competent chaplain to a bishop.

At that time you were an academic, and you'd had a go at being a seminarian. Very crudely, in terms of churchmanship within the Anglican communion, where would you put yourself?

I was very much on the sort of Anglo-Catholic right wing of the church then. I belonged to a very pious and august society called the Society of the Holy Cross, for priests who were within that tradition. I think I was changing my mind a little bit, because I was coming under the influence of Cambridge theologians such as Professor C. F. D. Moule who was my tutor at Cambridge. Much more important, I suppose, was the influence of C. H. Dodd and Michael Ramsey who were teaching then, plus friends like John Robinson, Hugh Montefiore, Simon Phipps and Bob Runcie. I suppose, liturgically and also from the point of view of 'praxis', we were middle-to-leg people in the Church of England, but really we were looking at questions and problems that belong, I think, to the more liberal middle scope of theology.

These were questions and problems of biblical scholarship?

Biblical scholarship; and also the possibility of putting out an apologia or philosophical – or at least an intelligent – apologia to the people who couldn't believe or who were hanging on by their eyelashes. As a result of going to Cambridge, I had my first experience of highly critical theology, where the negative results of the first half of the twentieth century's criticism – well, forty years – were still being mirrored in the Cambridge schools. There was very little positive theology, and of course no dogmatic theology, but I was lucky. I was saved from the doubt and despair that some of them had, because I had the marvellous good fortune to have Charlie Moule as my tutor. Also, when I was later doing an honours part of the tripos in New Testament, I had the help and advice of Professor Dodd and Professor Michael Ramsey. These three people came to deliver me from that appalling business of having to doubt the origins of the faith, of thinking that tradition was a bogus elaboration and imaginary falsification of the original simple brotherhood of man, etc., and the whole thing in question. Now, in a sense, I am glad I went through it.

Yes. But did the three men that you've mentioned –
C. F. D. Moule, C. H. Dodd and Michael Ramsey – give
you an example in terms of their Christian lifestyle? What
was it about them that impressed you?

Oh, undoubtedly first and foremost their Christian lifestyle. Secondly, their obvious scholarly integrity, matching the integrity of the rather negative critics. And also I think all three had a marvellous sense of the Holy Spirit's work in the Christian community, the church – not in any highly structured dogmatic sense, but nevertheless they had this idea of the Christian community reflecting and coming to grips with the inherent intellectual problems of theology within the doctrine of the church, and showing that there was a main line of consensus of Christians leading out into a respect for tradition, a respect for the scriptures that started it off.

This sounds like a peculiarly Anglican answer to an
Anglican problem.

Absolutely ...

... in that they were using the Anglican respect for tradition to fight back against those who had scoffed.

That's right. That is true. But one has to remember that Dodd, although he was *anima naturaliter Anglicana*, was a Congregationalist. And indeed, there were many Methodist, Congregationalist and Presbyterian scholars like D. M. Baillie and John Baillie his brother, who were pursuing that line. And the time of that tremendous defence of the Nicene faith against its critics produced, I think, in non-conformity in Britain, and in the national church in Scotland, a renewed sense of tradition. So it wasn't just a purely Anglican thing, though of course Anglican scholars from Lightfoot onwards had done the trick. And if I may just put a footnote to that: I believe the Church of Rome owes a great debt to those men. The Catholics weren't doing it with any kind of flair at that time in Britain, and the people on the continent who were doing it were in the doghouse.

Yes. The Dominicans.

We have to remember that. So Rome needs to have much more acknowledgement of the bulwarks put up for the faith by people outside her communion. And whatever I am now, I will never forego this debt of gratitude to those men and many of them before. I want all my Catholic friends to know that and appreciate it. They did the hard work. They kept out the floods. It wasn't the citadel stance of authoritarian dogmatism of Rome that kept it out. And we know that now, but we haven't quite acknowledged it.

Certainly Rome finds that hard to acknowledge.

Yes, but it jolly well ought to, and I will do my best while there's breath in my body to make them see this need for gratitude, which is an ecumenical virtue.

Did the social and political outworking of Christianity concern you at all at that stage?

Yes, it always concerned me because I was born into – well, not dire poverty, but the real thing I remember about my childhood was not only my parents' care for me, especially my mother's incredible self-sacrifice, but the fact that it was all done within complete poverty where there was no money in the house from Tuesday onwards, that sort of thing. So I always had a political thing, from about the age of 14, I had a political interest, in a way that my middle-class friends, who hadn't experienced that, weren't quite into; and even when they talked politically, I was aware that somehow or other they didn't know the experience of what it was like to be at the bottom of the pack.

Did your background and concerns influence them at all?

Yes, I was always regarded as a bit of a ... well, not a clown but someone who was amusing, someone who occasionally sparked off a bit of thought. By and large I didn't have much weight, either as scholarly weight or the sort of impressiveness that some of my friends had, who got diocesan jobs in the Church of England afterwards. At Corpus Christi, what I found most interesting was the one-to-one teaching at Cambridge – an hour with a student with an essay or something to talk about. I became rather famous for being able to 'crack' fundamentalists. And the deans of various colleges and theological lecturers of colleges would send me people to crack; this I did by dancing up and down on the sofa, saying how inspired the fourth redactor of the book of Amos was.

You were lecturing and tutoring at Corpus Christi. In any particular branch of theology?

Well, primarily in New Testament. For the university faculty, I used to do a short sort of general series of lectures on approach to the Bible, for first-year students, but my main teaching was in the college, with individuals reading theology from other colleges as well as my own.

St John's gospel played a quite important part in your ...

... Very much so, because at that time, C. H. Dodd had just produced his great work on the fourth gospel, and during that time, or perhaps a little before, R. H. Lightfoot had also produced a book on the fourth gospel. And of course at Corpus I had the particular office of the college of my predecessor one removed, Clement Hoskins, and his major work also was on the fourth gospel. The fourth gospel I would say within the 1950s at Cambridge was very much to the fore in New Testament studies and the interest of many people.

Now, without wanting to go down too long a side alley, about this time, you say you had dealings with fundamentalists. How would you comment on the Inter-Collegiate Christian Union and the Student Christian Movement state of affairs in Cambridge at that time?

Well, at that time, John Robinson who was Dean of Clare, Hugh Montefiore at Caius (I'm not sure) and I were all interested in what we called the 'church-in-the-college' movement, which meant that the chapel de-Anglicanised itself a bit so that it could cover more traditions than the one that was traditional with the college chapel set-up. My endeavour was to win the confidence of the Christian Union people so that they would come in with the SCM and everyone else, only not in some kind of college society but as the church, a people-of-God movement it really was.

Were you successful at all?

Well, success is very hard to measure, but, for example, we had perhaps a third or a quarter of the people who attended the regular meetings of the Christian Union coming to the chapel, which in some ways, given the rift between SCM and the Christian Union, was quite an achievement. Now, the whole business of SCM and Christian Union came up in the 1960s much more because what was going on in the 1950s – by which time the split between the SCM and the Christian Union had become settled – was that people seemed to be given an option between a vague non-commitment kind of religion which takes out what it feels to be relevant and leaves the rest, and a high-commitment faith which takes the Bible as it stands. Now, all my theological – and pastoral – life has been to try and find the transcending position, whereby you can have an honest critical use of the Bible combined with a high regard for its objective transcendent message, which is not ours, not man's word, nothing to do with 'relevancy' at all. In the 1950s, it was usual just to divide between the two polarised things, between a critical understanding of the Bible and a vague, discussion-kind-of-thing that went on – ridiculous SCM meetings whereby they discussed endlessly things that didn't require or didn't lead to any action; whereas the other lot were listening, on a rather naïve basis, to the Bible – but they did listen to it, and they heard the Word of the Lord to them, and they jolly well did it! And therefore tremendous admiration was due to the Christian Union people because they actually obeyed, in their own – perhaps, again, naïve – way, but they literally obeyed the things they heard from the Bible; whereas SCM made God into a problem.

So you were looking for the faith of one group combined with the critical awareness of the other.

Yes. Now, all my life I've been asking myself, how do you do this, where do you find it? Is it something that's possible? I mean, every movement in the church raises this question about the authority of the Word of God, whether it is about morals, or politics, or personal spirituality, or whatever it is. Are we listening to a voice that is not a human voice, or are we just left with a series of extraordinary documents issuing in the first century, or from the time of the Song of Moses and Miriam that the Old Testament began with? Have we got all this extraordinary roughage to go through before we can listen to what it says? All that, still, is a problem for the churches. But it was very, very polarised in the '50s, and even more so when SCM rather went down the drain, when it went in for all this complete process of secularisation and ended up in a dire thing, as we rather remember!

Going on through the 1950s, you were dealing with these problems. Are there any other dates or events in the '50s which you recall?

Oh yes. In the '50s, because of this search for authentic commitment which I was thinking out theoretically, as it were, I was also spending my long vacations looking round Christian groups and communities to see if I could pick up the authentic sound and voice and vibrancy of Christian commitment. And curiously enough, I found it most strongly among the French fraternities of the Little Brothers of Jesus. I brought back each year to Cambridge a rather donnish acquaintance with something that I could talk about, discuss and have meetings about, and I was becoming almost the authority on new movements in the Catholic Church. I realised what a danger it is to go around talking about somebody else's activities and not be really implicated in them myself. That began in 1954–5 onwards.

Where were these communities?

Well, at Anemasse, on the border between France and Switzerland, I visited a working fraternity of the Little Brothers of Jesus, and was highly impressed with their gutfulness, and two feet right into the whole business of the working man's culture. I was very impressed with their determination to stay in there for life, and very impressed with the simplicity and difficulty of their prayer programme

– and their hospitality, whereby on my first visit to the house, the Superior gave up his bed for me and slept in the corridor.

Does the liturgy here at Roslin, and the style of prayer, owe anything to those communities?

Yes. When we began at Roslin, I think one of the major intentions – though I don't know if it was all that thought out – was to provide Little Brother kind of vocations for non-Catholics, or at least for Anglicans, because there wasn't anything quite like that when we started out. That didn't change, but it was combined with all sorts of other things and it gave the Community a momentum in a way which, externally, may look away from the Little Brothers' particular patch. But yes, for example: there are two things in the Rule at Roslin, which really we owe entirely to the Little Brothers of Jesus. One is their Hour of Prayer as well as the Office; and the other is the saying of the Prayer of Abandonment of Charles de Foucauld each morning after Lauds – from which a whole spirituality has grown up which still makes sense to us.

This takes us on to the founding of your community, and we'll discuss that another time ...

3

RETURN *EMPTY* TO SCOTLAND
THE FOUNDING OF A COMMUNITY

So, Roland, let's talk about the beginnings of Roslin.
Could you give us more detail about how it happened?

Well, I'd already been a novice for two years at a religious
community (Kelham). When I got back to Cambridge, even
the pleasant, understandable, slotted-in life of a Cambridge
don didn't cover up, over the years, this yen I had for the
religious life. I didn't know what that meant, whether it
meant leaving Cambridge for an established community
or what, but in 1960 I suppose the community began as a
commitment of myself, when I was spending a retreat time
at Christmas in the monastery of Our Lady of the Cross at
Glasshampton, where Father William of Glasshampton had
gone initially to hope to set up a community of enclosed
contemplatives. He died alone as a hermit, and nobody
ever joined him, and his life was considered to have been a
bit of a failure by the people who want to see productivity.
So I went there – the house is now kept by the Anglican
Franciscans, but it's really designed for a contemplative
order that wants to return there, if anybody wants to use it.
One brilliant, cold, frosty December night, after Compline,
I wandered out into the cloister garden, and there, under
the crucifix of the cloister, is the grave of William of
Glasshampton; and, in the moonlight on that grave, I can

remember standing there and making a commitment to God. I don't know what it was about, but only that I would be prepared to leave anything I was doing, and anything I had, in order to follow up in some completely undefined way what Father William had been about. I didn't know what that meant; it was so vague that the conciseness of it was just in my saying to God that I would be prepared, if he showed me any way.

It was a submission.

Yes; saying, here I am. What for, goodness knows. But I knew it was something to do with that grave. And that resolution I made in 1960 is the first document of this community. So this, combined with the visits to the Little Brothers – the smallness of the thing. I was realising that, whatever I was going to do, it had to be precarious, it had to be fragile, not because it was the early stages of something that might grow into something big, but it had always of its nature to be fragile. And this was something that again was not thought out, it was a gut feeling about where the church was going to, and whether institutions and orders and big buildings, etc. etc., are part of the scene. It wasn't really thought out, it was just a gut reaction to what I thought was happening to the Christian existence in the new world that was shaping after the Second World War. Well, then I had two more years to go, doing this rather absurd job as Canon of Sheffield Cathedral. I was also running a kind of theological extra year for people who would voluntarily come to live with me, working in the steelworks of Sheffield, and talk about the questions that arose from their experience of working men's lives.

I beg your pardon, just to get dates clear here, Roland ...

It was 1958 I started. I was helping the students to do a sort of worker-priest thing, as an extra year to their rather posh training at Westcott House and Cuddesdon and various other places. By 1962, it was clear that the Church of England, whatever else was happening, wasn't particularly interested in that sort of thing. I would be going on doing that as a rather peripheral little experiment that wasn't really getting into the heart of training for the priesthood. And in my last year there, I was made very uncomfortable by the fact that I might just be left there doing this odd thing on my own, with my bishop's approval, but not with much effect on the general thinking of the Church. And the last year also produced one of the students who was living there, who said to me: 'I enjoyed my year with you in Sheffield, but of course, you're doing something that really isn't to do with the training of the ministry directly'. So I said: 'What do you mean?' He says: 'This – what you're doing – is really an experiment to something that ought to result'. So I said: 'What ought to result?' He says: 'Something like a community of some kind, I don't know what, something to do with community'. And this, combined with my Glasshampton experience, and the Little Brothers of Jesus – who had already settled in Leeds and we were very much close to them now – made me go to my bishop and lay all these things before him. And he said to me: 'Go off to Taizé. Go and spend three or four months in Taizé to find out if that's what you ought to do.' So I went.

Who was your bishop?

Bishop Leslie Hunter. He belonged to the Henson-Temple calibre of prophetic bishops.

So off you went ...

I went to Taizé – enjoyed it immensely – learned about how important it was to have ecumenical communities, not a one-little-flowerpot arrangement – learned, I think, to appreciate what was really being done in the Oxford Movement in the last century, because I saw it being done in quite a different scale, with quite different results, in Protestant France and Switzerland. There was an extraordinary basic quality of a return to a tough tradition. And all that affected me and drew me out, I think more than anything else, of the liberal influences of the Cambridge theology. So I owe Taizé a tremendous lot. The little Rule we live under at Roslin – which is a modification of the Rule of St Benedict – owes a great deal to Brother Roger's Rule for the brothers at Taizé. But halfway through that, it was clear – not to me, but to a strange Orthodox bishop, who told me – that I must return and take back what I'd learnt to Britain. However small whatever I was going to do, it must be done in Britain, because Britain never receives anything from the Continent, including Taizé, neat; it will always need a British translation. That was an Orthodox (Bulgarian, I think) bishop, staying at Taizé. So I got myself back again, but rather annoyed with God, because I didn't see anything in the British scene which was obvious. I'd been offered two jobs, both of which from the point of view of jobs were extremely enticing: one a fellowship at Merton College, Oxford, and the other to succeed – which I don't think I would ever have dared to do! – Father St John Grocer as Master of Saint Catherine's Institution in Stepney. That one was perhaps off-putting, but they were exciting possibilities to be thought about. And it was at just that time that the Bishop of Edinburgh, who was my great friend, Kenneth Carey, former Principal of Westcott House, Cambridge, who rang up Sheffield to say would I come up and look at this absurd chapel, Rosslyn Chapel. This seemed very far down the list from the job point of view, because there wasn't even a half-time job to be done there; it was this extraordinary chapel that was only used on Sundays and about three Holy Days a year, and the rest of the time was a museum. There was hardly any congregation; it was a little mining village, eight miles south of Edinburgh. And I would be moving into the Scottish Episcopal Church, a minority church that didn't seem to know what it was for. No, it was most unpromising!

Why do you think Kenneth Carey offered you this?

I think he offered it to me because, being one of my closest personal friends, he knew what was going on in my guts. And he knew, I think, that if I stayed down south of the Border, nothing would happen because I would go into a job-orientated choice. As a result of that, I would never gel with any companions but be always 100 per cent on the job. So he said: Come and do nothing and see what happens.

It was ridiculous, a chapel in the middle of nowhere, in the middle of a field – and a *museum*! I said to Ken Carey: 'What am I supposed to do with that?' He said: 'Preach the gospel and administer the sacraments'. And I said: 'What, amid all that? It's ridiculous!' So he said: 'Well, I want your answer in ten days, because the earl is getting rather worried. I've offered it to three dozen people before you, and this is scraping the bottom of the barrel!'

So when I went back, I went on that lovely train from Waverley through Carlisle, you know, the one that went all down through Hawick. When I got to Leeds City station, from Skipton – I remember I was praying to the Lord, and I was getting mad with him, and I was saying: 'Now Lord, I don't know what you're doing' – because I was 45! Was I? Yes. Ridiculous! So I said: 'Lord, you've got me where you want me, because I will do what you say as long as you make it perfectly clear to me what it is. I really don't mind what I do of all these things, but I will do anything as long as you make it clear: so jolly well get on with it.' That was the kind of prayer I was saying, when all of a sudden, coming out of Leeds the other way, was a big coal train, all of twenty trucks, and on the back, on the guard's van, it had a big notice – I've not seen one before or since. It was a paper notice, big red letters, and it said RETURN EMPTY TO SCOTLAND. The word 'Empty' was underlined. 'Right, Lord.' This event, on my return from seeing this highly unpromising little thing, is the only reason we're at Roslin. I mean, that is utterly irrational.

In what year did you go to Rosslyn Chapel?

I went in November 1962. I arrived in Roslin, to this huge cold house, the parsonage, a landmark on the Ordnance Survey map, the coldest and most unliveable house I've ever lived in, with a housekeeper – this huge place with a huge garden. I was wretched for the first six months until somebody came and said to me – when I was talking about my funny little bug of religious life and community as being a way to proclaim what we believe – 'What a good thing you've come here!' I said: 'What on earth d'you say that for? I've left all my friends south of the Border; and there is hardly any religious life.' There were about two convents for women in the Scottish Episcopal Church, none for men. He said: 'But you've come within twenty-three miles of a Cistercian monastery!' I said: 'I haven't!' He says: 'Yes, it's presided over by the most extraordinary man, a little Irishman called Columban Mulcahy, who is the chief promoter of ecumenism in eastern Scotland.' So from that day I picked up enormously, and went over and told him where I'd got to, and it was really him who encouraged me and fostered the beginnings of shape to the present community.

So you went to see Columban at Nunraw?

On several occasions between 1962 and 1965, and thereafter until he died. In fact, he was the first spiritual director of the community.

And those three years, 1962 to 1965, were years of staying in the parsonage, and gradually forming in your mind the possibility ...

... Yes, that's right. But I may say that the three people who were going to come to me – by the end of 1963 I thought I had on the hook three people who were going to come – all three came off the hook, and I was left another year and a half before Brother John offered to come, and we were able to begin.

Are you able to say who the three original people were?

No, because they've all got very good jobs, doing well, and probably I would say absolutely right, looking back on it.

Brother John is still with you.

Very much so.

John Halsey. Can you say a little bit about how he came to you, and what his search was?

Well, a very odd thing. Bishop Leslie Hunter had retired by then, 1964, and he invited a group of people who'd worked in his diocese – and that included John, who'd been with me in Sheffield – to meet with him, to discuss where next we went in the very puzzling 1960s, and I was given time to just say a few words about where I thought I was going to. When I got back, I found a letter from John, saying I don't know if it's anything to do with me, but if you felt it was all right, I think I'd be prepared to start up anything that's going on. And it was John who stuck, very much so, otherwise we wouldn't have been able to start. And then Robert Haslam, who stayed with us five years, came in, so there were three of us, in 1965. It was in 1965 that we moved out of the big house. We started there for the first three months, and then moved into this Miners' Institute place which we got for 800 quid.

What happened to Robert?

Robert was very interested in the Little Brothers of Jesus before he came. One good thing about this place is that it helps people sort out their vocations, and it was quite obvious that Robert was a loner. His real interest was certainly in the area of reducing the profile of ecclesiastical and 'religious' existence, so that we sank a little bit into the insignificance of the secular life and not into this wish to be important or to do something highly successful in the religious sphere. He'd got all that, but he could do it on his own, so after five years he found himself doing other things. He went off and became a goatherd, and had a goat farm, and he had a parish, then he went off to Charterhouse Centre in Southwark ...

... Now, Bishop Neil Russell came on the scene.

That's right. He came in 1968, from Africa, having retired from his bishop's job so that an African could take over. He was associated with us when he was in Africa, but when he came back, he came to try his vocation at the age of 63, in the Community, and he did it very successfully – quite extraordinary, a man who was obviously formed, mature, a leader, a very holy person. He managed to fit in with all this and was professed into the Community. He died in 1984 in Africa, where we had sent him back to be a hermit near a village where he could do some ministration; so we have a seed buried in African soil which I think would mightily influence where we would next wish to go, if the Lord ever sent us any more brothers.

Patty Burgess?

Patty was a member of the congregation of Rosslyn Chapel, that's where we met her. At that time she'd been a widow for some years, and now her family were grown up. She first of all became a deaconess, thinking that would satisfy her wish to be full-time in the Lord's service, but when she got to know the Community, she asked whether women could belong to this. Well, we'd always had a kind of hope that there would be a women side to all this. Whether it was going to be a mixed community we didn't know, but we took Patty on board and she joined the Community in 1972, but living on her own. In 1975, she moved to Roslin because she needed to live in community; so for a time we were a mixed community, as it were. But after taking advice and looking at mixed communities, which by that time had sprung up in one or two forms, we decided – and certainly

Patty was as decided about that as we were – that we should be contiguous, but not geographically on the same spot. Patty moved to Loanhead, to the flat that Robert Haslam had when he moved out of Roslin. She lives the same life, the same Rule, the same structure of life, but lives it on her own. How she does it I do not know. She has, from time to time, people who try their vocation to this extraordinary life. So Patty has had a very hard furrow to plough for many years now.

When was it that Patty and you came to this decision?
About 1976.

Now, I'd like to ponder on this a little bit, because of course, having separate men and women communities very much goes against the modern grain, and yet I find it echoes something to do with Saint Francis and Saint Clare: separateness, and yet a deep communion of the heart. Could you tell us a bit about that?

Let it be said that one of the obvious reasons why we couldn't really see ourselves going on with more than one fairly elderly widow as sisters was that it would be fairly impossible, because of at that time highly primitive bathroom arrangements – one loo, the whole thing's lived on a postage stamp. The contiguity is so close here that it's impossible really to live the monastic life with the two sexes cheek by jowl. It just isn't physically possible. If we'd had a larger thing, almost certainly we'd have had something like a double monastery, like Turvey in Bedfordshire, where they've got two houses, and common use of the Chapel, but we just hadn't the physical amenities to allow the possibility of a close-range unity. But going on to your point, I think this is terribly important. In the '60s and '70s, and even now, the whole mood is to have no distinction whatsoever; but as we think of the psychology, and even more of the theology, of the sexes, it seems to be the complementariness, and not identity, of communities and the sexes which is most important. These are the things which give maximum life; as long, as you say, as there's a Clare–Francis balance, and not the old pattern of the existence of the female orders with very little influence with the male side of the order – especially, the females having to sit down under the dictates of the male side of the order. It still happens in some of them. So we have this business of togetherness on the one ticket, and yet a freedom. I think a freedom, too, in relation to the kinds of people and the work we do; there's a kind of freedom given to the layman and the cleric to come into a house of one or the other, which is different from a mixed group, and it wins in the end. I don't know how to define this, and it's an area which we haven't really thought out, but there's a kind of freedom when people know the category of the house they're going to, and they adapt themselves accordingly. That isn't to say that all males go to us and all the females go to Patty, but there's a sense in which they know the nuances of a house.

There would be some radical Christians who would accuse you of sexism.

I think they would have every right to do so, if we felt that the men's house was either superior to, or dictating to, or doing anything to transgress the utter freedom of the sisters to get on with what they'd got to do.

I want to ask you a theme question rather than a history question now, and it's about ambition. You mentioned the theme of wanting to do something important in the church and in religious life. Now, having had all these lives, in Sheffield and Cambridge – academic life, having met people who became household names, like Runcie and Robinson and Dodd who influenced you – and having been in positions of power and then having given it all up when you came here to Roslin, were there ever times when you thought: I've got to carry on and do something?

Oh! yes. They occur now. You see, there's one parable in the gospel, which I think is open to misuse, because it's a parable that comes out and haunts you, and that's the parable of the talents, which of course is so agreeable to competitive capitalism. And the whole of the social order is on the side of the man who develops, fulfils his existence, by a stretched life of activity and concern which becomes developed to the full – something that people can see, and take account of, and get inspiration from, and even be affected by. In the watches of the night, I am still haunted by this awful thing, this awful voice, which says: 'Haven't you arranged to live in a tin shack, in a hen hut in the garden, so that you can escape the responsibilities that you refused when you turned down jobs that would have led to important things?'

The voice says: 'You could have changed the church for the better'?

Why yes, the voice says all sorts of things. When he says that, of course, I know where it comes from. I know that's the devil's mark, when he says that. So he doesn't often say that. He's subtle. He's saying: 'Didn't you dig a hole and hide your talent, by arriving at a scruffy mining village and staying there, when there was everything to do, and you left your brothers with the hard labour of the sweat and heat of the day?'

And how do you answer?

How do I know whose voice it is? How do I know that I haven't transferred my ambitions from being 'Someone' – which I could never be in the academic world? Perhaps it was my knowledge of my limitations in that world, where I only just held a very humble job academically. Perhaps I also learnt my limitations by knowing that the administrative work beyond the work of a canon in a cathedral was something I couldn't attempt. Perhaps I changed my tune, and I've still got ambitions to be

Somebody who's now regarded as Somebody who's Done the Right Thing, who's now shown the way by his humble demission of opportunities; and is now the prayer man, the guru! Who knows about these things? What do I actually do when that happens? And it happens more often than one would think. I think I go back to Paul's words that 'I judge not my own self', and I certainly am not going to be judged by anyone else. My whole judgement must wait until the Judgement Day, and I shall be judged, like everybody else, not on how much I've done in the sense of work that's worthy of being written up and remembered, but whether I fed the poor when they came, and whether I clothed the naked. Well, I can only say this: that in my weakness, I need to live a form of life where at least the chances of doing that – I'm not saying they're always taken – are more frequent than if I took on jobs that would have hermetically sealed me off from access of the poor. Matthew 25 is our only justification of where we are going to, and even then we don't know how to judge ourselves because we don't even know when we are doing this, apparently, according to Matthew 25. But that's the only thing to come back and rest on: the Day of Judgement, equally for everybody, will be about that sort of thing. Therefore one has to give up this attempt at justification; but if the temptation is so much that we weakly need to justify what we are, I would only say that the movement into this kind of craziness enables me, at least, to be within more range of the distress of the world than I would have been – I'm not saying this is true of everybody who takes high office – if I'd gone up some ladder. That's the kind of thing that occurs to me. But if your question is '*Did* I ever?', it's '*Do* I ever?', and the answer is: 'Many, many times this comes to me', because from the point of view of friends and people who perhaps don't always see the point of other people's decisions, they still challenge me. It's not only voices in the night. Friends can still challenge me. They say: 'What on earth do you think you're doing up there?' – because if anybody goes to

Scotland, for a start, it's supposed by an Englishman to be handing in your chips.

You mentioned the Little Brothers earlier on. They've obviously had an influence on the formation of this community. Tell us some more about that.

Well, Brother John's vocation to this Community then – and still does – contained a tremendous proportion of wanting to follow out the inspiration of Father René Voillaume and the Little Brothers of Jesus. We have to be self-supporting, and each of us in turn has had to go out and earn a living for the Community. Brother John from the start has always had jobs at the bottom of the pack. He was a trained miner, then he became a priest-workman, and then when the local mine closed here, he started working at a local car-renovation place, a Ford subsidiary, where he prepared, at a basic labourer's wage, cars for spraying and panel-beating. He has to scrub the rust off the cars, and just do menial jobs. And that is very much along his personal vocation. And one good thing about the history of our little group is, we've been able, up to now, to find the right levels and flexibility of fulfilling the personal vocation within the general vocation of the Community. That's become very important, as we had a critical view of what happened to monasteries. On the whole, the monk in the bigger monasteries was certainly assigned his work according to what he could do, and his physical and mental capacities; but, because the work was always undertaken on the spot, there was and still is a sense in which there's a limitation to the kind of work a monk can be put to. If you translate what needs to be done in the monastic tradition – namely that the monk himself must find ways of being economically and socially inserted into the society he lives in, so that he almost certainly in the future will have to have work outside the poor, constricted, postage-stamp size of his house – then this flexibility is inevitably to come through more modern experiments. In renovations of old orders, it's already coming to pass.

And this is the René Voillaume vision?

That's right. He had already seen that, and had got it going; and we imitated it, we would still imitate it. We are not allowed to accept money, or live in property of the church. The abbot of Nunraw was very insistent that we should be self-supporting, to follow this part of the Little Brothers' vocation. On the other hand, it's got to be said that as we associated ourselves with the Cistercian order, we discovered that there was a kind of momentum that is still in process within the community, to look at and adapt – but to keep – certain monastic elements that the Little Brothers of Jesus, for the purpose of what they want to say and do, have had to forego. For example, in this community there is a threefold pattern. The abbot of Nunraw was quite insistent that we should look at the gospel life of Christ, because Benedict himself said it was a school for the gospel life. We should look at the gospel life, we should also look at the monastic tradition and save bits of the tradition which are recognisably part of the gospel life. We found that the gospel life of Christ consisted of three aspects. First is his communion in solitude with his Father. Therefore, however small the community is, it must provide somewhere geographically where the brothers or sisters can go into solitude. And solitude has become a very definitive part of our life, where we would say that one of the riches that we have recovered for ourselves is this need for the contemporary rightness – relevance, if you like to use that awful word – of solitary life. So we've got a part of the little tiny bit of property fenced off into silence, where the brothers actually live, and if they've got no reason to be anywhere else, they're in their separate cells in the garden, which is an enclosure. It also contains the chapel. Now, the accessibility of the community is in the house of hospitality, where you can have the poor, you can put up your guests, and you can have the kind of Lord's public house and food and everything all together. And that corresponds to this ever-present company of the apostles, which must have bored the Lord stiff, to always have to be with that group. Lastly, there is the issuing to outside where you make the occasional – and certainly I would say getting smaller and smaller – forays into church and society for meetings and togethernesses of other kinds. That's becoming less and less. Going out to prop up other bits and pieces of what other people are doing is becoming less because the work on the spot is growing, and there's a dearth of vocations anyway, and the concentration is much more on people coming to us, rather than we going to them.

To go back to the gospel life of the Lord, which is the root of all this. Presumably the Lord's interaction with Jerusalem is the pattern for your Community's interaction with the church?

Yes, in a way. Let's say, first of all, that Jesus gave us the rule about adhesion to the church: that is to say, you stay in until you're chucked out. You never chuck yourself out. And that's been a fundamental thing of our Community. We will always have the closest love, like the Lord had for the city, so that we hope to weep occasionally over Jerusalem.

As indeed you do, when you're not laughing.

Exactly! Is that right?

And also of course, Jerusalem is the place of the Lord's crucifixion.

That's right. Therefore we have always maintained – to the point of seeming conservatism by other groups that have been formed at our time or since – the highest respect for the authority of the church. We have a Visitor, now appointed jointly by the Roman Catholic Cardinal and the Anglican Bishop of Edinburgh. We have, as well, from a religious community, usually a contemplative monk or nun who is our warden. That is to say, he or she represents to us the guide and pattern, the one who would determine the pattern and mood of the community, so that it doesn't fall outside the tradition – not the traditions, but the tradition – of the church. She is there to ascertain that we don't do anything that is outrageously out of line with the Spirit's growth within the community of the church. And therefore for example, it says in the Rule – which is very difficult to know how to put this, of course, from the point of view of an ecumenical community – let nothing be done without the consensus of the church! Now, lawyers could make hay of that; but it means that we are not here to be some strange off-beat lot of people who are negatively either knocking everything that's happening or on the other hand positively going at speeds which no church which claims the name Catholic could really underpin. On the other hand, of course, no-one's going to exist with any authentic gospel existence within the church that doesn't suffer with the church and because of the church and through the church. The human side of the institution will cause any devout lover of the Body of Christ to be anxious, pained, distressed. In fact, that's the mark of a true lover of Christ's Body. So we have to endure all this, on this tightrope between oddness of living and a profound affection and regard for what is, historically, all the Lord has – his people. And there we contribute just as much – in fact, perhaps a higher percentage – of nonsense to the general body as anyone else is producing. So we've got to be humble, but on the other hand, modestly discerning and awake to what can harm and defeat the gospel life of Christ within the church. It should be difficult; it always was, it seems to me. How Paul was able to manage to be in that fellowship with Peter – as we know, it was in danger from time to time – how they all got on together, it's a miracle of Pentecost that all these extraordinary people of the New Testament got on together. So we've got to return to this, rather than this ridiculous unthinking subservience to authority that occasionally can be, and certainly is, misused from time to time. We've got to let this type happen. And I think that goes for every bishop, pope, and everybody in the church.

You said a while ago that your going out, and doing talks and so on, was diminishing rather; is that deliberate?

It is rather inevitable, because if you've only got three people living this life, for one to be absent is a fantastic thing. It's not like a big community where you can send somebody out, and it doesn't make any difference – you don't even know he's gone! Here it's just a gap, and certain work is not done that's being sent here. We've undertaken to look more closely at, and be more attentive to, the work that's being sent here, rather than what people are asking of us, because the work that's sent here is much more given from God than the pulls and tugs from all sorts of little movements in the church that always want you to be interested in what they're doing. Slowly, they will pull you away from what you're doing. We've found that over the years. From time to time, the danger was that we had every attention on what everybody else was doing, and nobody thought about what was happening here. What happens in this house is the most important thing, after what happens in the enclosure. So when we've got time, or when there's a house full of people who can undertake the life of the house, okay; but otherwise, let's look at the importance of this togetherness, and the resources of shared living of the life, rather than this going about all over the place. And the other point is that we've discovered – which other people have discovered before us, of course – that the church today is full of meetings and conferences, to a point of frenzy. We need now to damp it down rather than to stir it up.

Too much talking?

Oh, infinitely! Especially about prayer!

*I remember you writing and speaking about the threefold
cord of simplicity, joy and compassion which you found
coming to you from the gospel, and the sources you've
mentioned other than that, like Charles de Foucauld –*

And Taizé, above all.

*I can see the compassion, in what goes on here in the
house; I can see the simplicity, in the enclosure; I have to
look a little harder to see the joy.*

The joy bubbles up from the fact that it's all like shovelling
sand, it's the joy of people who aren't going to get anywhere!

Isn't that confusing joy with sick laughter?

No, it isn't. It's a marvellous joy to know that God can
use the complete non-entities and insignificancies of life.
That is a joy beyond all compare, because it's really back
to where the incarnation is, back to the little nonsense
which produces the gospels. It's all about insignificance,
it's all about nothingness being used, it's the joy of the
Magnificat. Not some incredible, marvellous professional
serenity. It's a great laugh at the nonsense that God can
do something with. Is that right? Do you experience that
here?

*Yes, I see. I, as an outsider, find that very difficult to
experience and appreciate, because I have not surrendered
my position in the world, and I haven't stepped outside
and I haven't turned upside down to see things the way
God sees them. I'm like the vast majority of Christians,
and let's face it, the vast majority of people in this country,
in that respect.*

On the other hand, I've seen your joy at the very
insignificancies of life in your family. Your joys spring out
of the ridiculousness, of the insignificance and fragility of
the nonsense that God has given to us. You have the same

joy; you get it in your family, I get it here. But it's the same joy. Knowing that the insignificant is significant to God. That is tremendous. That is the basis of joy. Is it?

Seeing things from the worm's-eye view of God.

In effect, the devil can never remove that joy, because we've got so much of it. The joy isn't the fact that we're doing anything we can write home about. It's the joy that comes out of what the Lord does with the nonsense.

That's a very monastic thing.

Yes, I think so, but the Lord finds joy in what he creates. In what *he* creates, says the Psalmist. Is that right? We find our joy in seeing him do it. You say it's very monastic, but this is where I would want to disagree, because unless the monastic life is pointing to, is indicating, the simplicities of Christian living to everybody, it's liable to become – and historically did become – professional. A monk to my mind is a person who is discovering for himself, and for the rest of Christians, his basic humanity. He's got nothing else. He shouldn't have. He should only have what he is like as a human being when everything is reduced to almost nothing. And he should not be doing that for himself, as his own way to heaven, or as part of some professional phalanx of SAS troops within the church, but just indicating simply: find out what it is that you are when all that you seemingly have, and can do, and achieve is removed, as it will be. If somebody said to me: 'What in essence do you think you're doing by this ridiculous life? Why didn't you join an order? Why did you start this, when there's so many of these things wanting novices for this and that? Was it because you just wanted to do it yourself? Or was it because you wanted to say something?' Well, God wanted to say something. But I think if anybody asked *me* that sort of question, I would say: we wish as far as possible, given the history of all our institutions within the church, to live as unprofessionally as possible, because one of the blights of monastic life, when it's let go, is it becomes a *profession*, and in its own way a club, with its own language. It's done the very reverse of what our fathers in the desert, and Benedict himself, wanted to do – just give a chance to simple, average and less-than-average men to live the life of the gospel. If it's more than that, if it's pushing oneself up into being 'Somebody' within the church, then let's have done with it. Is that right? What lovely stuff, it's crazy! It is crazy, isn't it!

Can you tell us about the physical conditions of being a monk here? It's the middle of winter, and it must be quite a hard life.

Well, it's all comparative, obviously. But let's look at what is really rather a continual problem with monasticism. As Hans Kung says, Christ was certainly not a monk. He may have had, through John the Baptist, certain vague knowledge of and perhaps visits to, Qumran, which was a Jewish form of monasticism, a rather austere one. But Christ set his face against any removal from the world, any *fuga mundi*, any flight from the world. And he was found well outside the religious context of professional Judaism, mixing with publicans and sinners, just mucking in apparently, and letting life happen around him and rather casually picking up people and situations in a – to our minds, perhaps – seemingly ineffectual way, day by day. But with all that, there is Christ the man who is ready to give up home, to give up domestic comforts, and even ready to describe himself as one who hasn't got anywhere to lay his head; and of course, the influence on Christian spirituality of the Passion makes it certain that as soon as the church is not persecuted, there is going to be a revival of some high commitment. So monasticism was in fact an inevitable consequence of a rather easy-going living church in the cities of the Hellenistic world. The Egyptian beginnings of monasticism were very austere and had a kind of poverty that was only seen in medieval Europe with Francis – who again took the words literally from the gospels and led this fantastic and impossible life which was antisocial in one sense, and yet itself was the source of things which happen even to this day, which has implications for society. So there's always this ambivalence about monasticism and the gospel; and yet a kind of inevitability that any full expression of the church's spirituality, in every age, seems to demand a monastic factor.

So you're saying that monasticism exists almost outside the church; and yet the church needs it?

Yes. By its very nature it's a marginalised life. It's going away from the pressure scenes, and where things seemingly happen, into a kind of non-happening existence, where things begin to happen over which you don't wish to have – or shouldn't have – control. You create a space within the busyness of life so that something else – many things – happen; but they're not under your control, and they're given to you, as it were, quite unorganisedly. In other words, what I think monasticism is about is creating a space where 'it came to pass' – which is quite frequently quoted in the Bible – can happen again and again. Now, this is to put your sights wholly in 180 degrees from the modern culture, where control – effective management, and all that – is the great hallmark of successful and responsible living. So the monk always looks like an irresponsible man; he's not answering in the way society expects.

This is the desert, isn't it?

Yes, the desert part of it.

But can you tell us, why is physical hardship so important to this desert?

Well, I think for a modern reason – I don't think this really enters into the insights of the first monks – a modern impulse towards simplicity of life and to rather make-do-

and-mend situations, which is really what a monk is trying to do: just be content with what he's got, and not keep on wanting anything that he hasn't got. And only supplying what he knows to be necessity, because he is more conscious today of the fact that 50 per cent of the human race lives under par from what we consider to be necessities of life. They just haven't got them, and aren't likely to have them, and getting more likely not to have them. So there's a social impulsion, or should be, in monasticism. Perhaps I can go on to say something about where I think monasticism is going to, and where it's got to, and whether we're doing it. You mentioned cold. This house is all we've got, and it was produced in a rather extraordinary way, 100 yards from where we were living when we started. We started in a big commodious house, the biggest in the village, and we knew we had to get out of that, to make any sign to ourselves or to anyone else. There was this extraordinary rusted and dilapidated corrugated-iron Miners' Institute, which nobody wanted, and in fact everybody thought in the village that it would be taken down and a house built on the spot. We hadn't much money. I had £400 saved, and so did Brother John. So that made £800. So we went round to the woman who owned the property and asked her what she wanted for it, and she said £800! That was all we had, so we paid it and got the key. Then we had the awful thing of the church, in the person of the bishop – whom we had to obey – and also we couldn't spend any money without his permission. He came and looked at it, and he says: 'Good gracious, I wouldn't let a dog live in there'. So we said: 'Would you let us get it, and see what we can do with it in six months, and then you can come back and have a look at it and see if you'd let us live in it then?' And he thought he was winning by saying okay because we had no money. Then we had another sign that we should be doing this. There was a man in the village who was quite well-heeled – he was a tea-planter – who passed by while we were trying to do something with the garden, which hadn't been touched for about fifteen years.

He says: 'What are you doing there?' We said: 'Well, we're going to live in it'. 'I'll give you £500 to do that place up', he says. And £500 in 1965 was quite a lot of money. So in we went, asked the bishop back in six months, and there we were. Well now, the very getting of the house, and the very fact that we had to make do and mend for what we'd got to live in, meant that we were really put on the track of making-do-and-mend being the incentive, the principle of everything we were up to. And slowly we became conscious of the fact that if we ever grumbled about not having what we thought we needed, we were reminded that we were very much nearer – though only a few centimetres more than anybody else – to the plight of everybody else who has to make do and mend in the human race. So this business of monasticism and austerity – which I think is not the word because we've got full bellies and we survive and we've got many things like books and running water and hot water and all the rest of it, things that are really luxuries – but this living, learning not to want anything more than you've got, is really a principle which comes from the gospel: of living in the present, not having projects to get more and more, not to think man's life consists in the abundance of things he has, and all the rest of it. So I would say people come here – most of them come as young people who want the experience of something a little odd – and they stay, sometimes for a year, sometimes for as long as two years. But, at the end of the day, commitment to this kind of life I don't think will be very much in evidence. We've only had five life professions. And we were warned by our warden that we weren't to expect many; if we had three all at one time we would be doing right, and probably almost certainly fulfilling the inspiration behind our dedication to the Transfiguration. There were three, and there always have been three. Never any more committed people.

So at least that way you'll avoid the fate which befell the Franciscan community!

Well yes, but by a rather back-handed way, of not being able to succeed!

But this again is something at the heart of monasticism.

Yes. You see, here's a funny story. We had the most back-handed compliment paid us when a friend of ours, whose own friend had been through a rather bad mental breakdown, came out and said could we take this man, because he wanted a place to recover from what he had been through. And I said to him: 'But your pal, he's used to creature comforts, he would hate this, damp rooms, bed linen not dried out properly, it's impossible', I said. He says: 'No, I've been told by the psychologist-man that what he needs is a place where people have failed!' He says: 'Your place is the only place I can think of!' Now, isn't that beautiful? Which raises this whole problem of 'success' in the business of Christian spirituality. Again, it's terribly hard to take on board this absence of success.

And yet, curiously and conversely, it's when you have turned your back on those values that somehow your very detachment from them has an effect on the world, doesn't it?

Yes.

Monasticism has always had an effect on the church and the world, and so your existence here, and your lack of efficiency, your lack of management values and lack of regard for the way society conducts itself, has in fact had an effect on the church.

Well, yes and no. If you read the gospels, Christ obviously didn't set out to found a world religion in a highly successful way, like Christianity. I think we're all getting to know that he's not the founder of Christianity – in spite of the fact that C. H. Dodd, one of the greatest of people who opened up for us the New Testament, called his last book *The Founder of Christianity*. I'm not sure it's a title that really suits the book ...

... Or the man.

Or the man. Because it seems to me that Christ was looking around for an elite. A back-to-front elite, who would follow him, and who would become because they were small – you didn't want a plateful of them – the salt of the world. It was all for the rest of them. But he didn't, I don't think, at any time, give you the impression that he was out to found a highly successful, potent religion that's going to be one of the world's five great religions. I don't think that was the way he thought. What he saw was that, if you got some people to live the reverse of what everybody else was, then you might have a little effect, which nothing else could have because everybody else is on the other thing. And I think monasticism, in a funny sort of way, has got this idea that they've got to be there for the rest. Now, they haven't historically always been there for the rest, because they made themselves into clubs. In fact, the curse of monasticism is when you create a club out of what should be an open-ended relationship to the rest of society. Monasticism on the whole, I think, has always been a prey to two temptations. One is to become, cosily, a club of identifiable, uniformed members that have a certain status, even, within the church, and are revered, and get a lot of kudos because they seem to be on the first-class ticket and the rest are going on second-class. Now, that's a terrible temptation, which even here we have to fight against. For example, in the question of wearing a habit. A habit is a very useful thing. We are given it at profession and we're proud of it, because it connects us up historically with our movement within the church, and in other religions, the Buddhists etc., where we're proud to have a family of peoples to whom we belong. But if that habit becomes the uniform of specialisation, of expertise, even of spiritual expertise, then it's defeated its purpose. So we don't wear the habit outside of offices of the church, and even then it's not an obligation.

So the one temptation is to be a club.

That's right. The other temptation, of course, is to be brought inside by the establishment of the church, to be tamed as it were, as an instrument of the present-day level of the faith or the spirituality of the mass of the people. That again is sinister, and we have to resist it, and sometimes it's very painful. You have to make it perfectly clear to the organised, institutional church that you're there – obviously part of them and couldn't live without them, and we're very particular, in this place, because we're so small, of relating very carefully in obedience to and in reverence for the authorities of the churches as an ecumenical little thing – but on the other hand, we daren't be brought in, either to manage parishes or to prop up what's there. We've got to keep on being marginalised. And that's sometimes quite painful, because the institution doesn't always understand what you're there for. So you've got these two temptations – either being tamed, or yourselves becoming cosily clubbable. In the past, we've had this appalling history of monasticism, where they've given themselves out as having the first-class ticket, and the laity and the secular priesthood being something quite subordinate or not so good.

Or even, in some theologies I seem to remember, not saved at all.

Right. In fact, the calling of the monastic profession a 'second baptism', for example, is a terrible thing – as if the first baptism didn't take for general folk, and you had to have a second one really to get in. Terrible stuff!

4

HOW TO BE A MINISTER
WITHOUT REALLY TRYING

*What advice would you have for the ordinary minister and
priest in terms of what to concentrate on? Given the fact
that the obsession with statistics is a burden, and also that
the way of the crusades and the big evangelists isn't the
right way, what should be happening at the parish level?*

This involves something that every old man does. An old
man says to himself: 'If I had my life over again, what
would I have done with it?' And I do this probably more
often than I should. I say to myself: 'What are the things
I have expended energy on – looking back on it, rather
useless energy?' I would say it was in trying to make sense
of the situation – let's call it the institutional situation of
the church – and trying to, as it were, make it tick. Now,
the church obviously isn't basically an institution, though
it can't go down through history without some kind of
wheels which turn out to be, historically and socially,
quite institutional. I'm not going to knock the institution,
because I believe that the church has to be incarnated into
ordinary rough-and-tumble history, and not just simply be
a group of elite people who in some kind of absolute purity
of conviction do their stuff and hand it on to another lot
of elite people. But, with regard to the organic nature of
the church, that is to say, being Christ's body, where it is

incarnate in the flesh and blood and the lives and nerves of ordinary people, I would like to have thought that my energy was going into making sure that the *life of Christ* was springing up in the person and in the community, rather than doing a lot of tinkering about with how the institution saw itself.

So, coming back to your question, I would say that my life has, as it were, funnelled down from a great interest in the total circumference of the church – its historic existence in the human scene – to this whole business of prayer. I'm old-fashioned enough to believe – along with many nineteenth-century Scottish ministers who, if you read their biographies, really did give attention to their life of prayer – that this is what truly matters. If I had anything to say to the average minister, I would say this: *Concentrate on enabling people to encounter God.* One might say: 'Well, that's obvious'; but underneath all the plethora of busy activity of the minister's life there's this crying need of the person, and then through the person into the community, and through the community to the person. There is this obvious knowledge of the believer that everything that matters springs from God, from the doing of his will to the knowing of God: and for the loving of God, and appreciating what God's doing, rather than what *we* are up to. It comes back to that initial thing we talked about – the difference between faith and religion. So I would say: 'What are the things within parish life that are accessible to the minister and the people to encourage the meeting with a living God who is active not just within the pieties and the orderings of the church's life, but can be perceived and embraced by their social and political and communal existence as human beings?' But that discernment and that encounter depends upon what I call prayer – which is not necessarily lots of words and doing things. And it is the nature of this prayer that I am more interested in than perhaps anything on earth. What is the kind of prayer that is quickly and securely available within the church's life –

communal and personal – which enables the individual and the community to daily, weekly, together, encounter God as a living, active person? If there's any truth in that, then it means saying to the average minister: 'Look, you may have thought, you may still think, that you are a "minister of religion", and sometimes in official documents this is how you are asked to describe yourself'. I refuse point blank ever to call myself a 'minister of religion'. I think that religion, like anything else that is human, is full of bugs and on the whole is not worth the candle, because it is about some self-preoccupation with what I am doing for God. And usually it's damn-all. This is what defeats us: we know it doesn't amount to very much, and so we've got this terrible crushing conscience that we're ministers of religion but we haven't got much of it ourselves – and yet we're trying to whip it up in other people. And this is a dead loss. But if you go on to the other business of seeing, loving, living, meeting, and all these great words of human existence, something happens because that is something God is going to do. It's *God* who is going to open our eyes and open our ears, to show himself. All the initiative is from God's side, it's not something we can turn on. So prayer is not first of all an activity whereby we are going to brush ourselves up and be somebody. We are going to be the passive receivers of something we need. Prayer in the Eastern Orthodox tradition is beautifully described as 'standing naked before God'. Just imagine, you can display all your warts and all your wounds and let him start on the healing and curing. So I would say to any young man or woman who is entering the ministry at present: 'Concentrate first of all on what God has already done for you, for your community, for where you live, and watch God doing something'. In a paradoxical way, I've moved over, for twenty-odd years now, perhaps thirty years, to this *attention*. I mean severe attention to the openness, passivity, empty-handedness of the human being. Whether he knows it or not, that is what it means to be a human being – a poor soul or an old dear.

You're either one or the other. And to try and cover that up is the exercise of human activity – to make quite sure that you're not a poor dear and you're not an old soul. Culture, and I would say church activism, enables us to go on with the illusion that we can stand before God as his strong people, and be somebody.

There are an awful lot of ministers and priests who, when they wake up in the morning, feel despair. There's tremendous pressure there because, if you're engaged in perpetual activity to achieve this cover-up, in actual fact the activity isn't all that much valued now, and it's done by a diminishing band of people.

Yes, you have this syndrome of more and more activity involving less and less people. In any other business, the management would take over at this point and say: 'Look, this is going into the ground', wouldn't they? I don't see at present the institutional management of the church saying: 'This has got to be attended to because this means death – real death for the people doing it'. It can drive them crazy or it can make them pack up, or have breakdowns or just move on to certain tramlines which they can find manageable. And all those very active resolutions of a real difficulty lead nowhere. They're hopeless. And it's this hopelessness that is the despair of the minister waking up in the morning. It's a form of despair because the human condition isn't really related to what he or she is doing. It's not just a question of Christian stuff, it's a question of the minister or priest as a *human being*. It's not as if we're dealing with a professional malaise, as some articles in the church papers seem to imply – the burnt-out case and all the rest of it. They're not digging deep enough to see the real problem is that the ministry, worked on those kind of principles, is out of line with the human condition of the man or woman.

And so there is a contradiction at the heart of all this?

This contradiction sets up a kind of imprisonment in something that cannot on its own terms be resolved. And the ministers know that. Deep down, there's this awful cry of anguish and then despair. And that's why the reversing of the whole process is necessary before you start. And that's where this prayer business comes in. Not prayer as another kind of *activity*. If you're not careful, you can do this the wrong way. I have found that I can go to a clergy conference and pour out my soul about this prayer stuff, and then you find that what you've done is put another load of heavy stuff on to already burdened people.

Because they already feel inadequate, and you then add spiritual inadequacy as well?

That's right. Whereas the whole business about prayer comes from that one great text of the Eastern Orthodox icon, as Christ presents the book to the people with blessing and command: 'Come unto me all that travail and are heavy laden and I will give you rest'. Good life, that's what they need – and do they ever get any? The beloved disciple is invited to lean back on the shoulder of Christ, as Christ rests in the bosom of the Father. All this is *given* – it's sheer gift. But unless you do that, prayer can look like another damned activity!

The other side of the coin, Roland, is that if the minister were concentrating on prayer, a lot of people would see that as laziness. The whole modern ethos is to achieve. 'Are we paying that person to sit up there not doing anything? It's our hard-earned money. Why is the minister not out there doing a schedule of forty visits a week and organising ten meetings?'

This is an incredible 180-degree reversal of what it's primarily about. You get this awful productivity culture demanding – literally demanding – that the minister is seen to be producing something in the way of pew-filling or fulfilling a schedule. In fact, some of the churches have literally sent round forms for ministers to fill in how they spend their time.

Yes, time management. And if you're not actually out there on the job, running around frantically and overburdened ...

... and *seen* to be the great assiduous attenders of committees! You get kudos from your fellow clergy if you do that. 'He never misses a single meeting ...' I've heard that again and again. What a waste of a life! I mean, it's a form of purgatory. That's one thing, they'll never have to do any time in purgatory, these poor ministers – they've done it. They'll go straight to heaven! Look at all these marvellous gifts of the spirit. In the New Testament: it's all about lining up with your empty hands to be *given* something. And really the *doing* side of it all, when you look at the New Testament, it's not all there. There is a sense in which Luke–Acts is a bit of an ideal picture of the church going out and conquering the Roman Empire. These remarkable men of the first century could write up that vision, but I do think that Luke–Acts gives a bit of leeway to those people who want to get us all steamed up about something. The spread of the faith is something that has to go on – but how? And with what methods? Does it mean the frenzy of the secular propagandist? What kind of peace do we bring to this world, and do we bring it within our ministry? Is it a gift, or is it something that we psychologically have to stir up by certain techniques and all that? Again you've got activism coming in as a kind of psychologism, a spoilt spirituality. The living of faith can be mucked up by an overactive self-interest in the techniques of how I'm going to be this beautiful prayerful person. And with all these second- and third-hand little books on spirituality, you're hoping you're going to find one which you can manage to get cracking on – when in actual fact anything that stripped you of any illusion about yourself and what you're going to do would be far better than all this guff about these lovely people who are going to be produced by certain spiritual exercises.

The irony is that achievement can penetrate the whole spirituality thing, like: 'How are you getting on with your prayer life?' 'Well, actually rather well. I find the time goes very quickly.' While another wee guy despairs and thinks: 'How am I going to get through this?'

I almost have nausea when I think about having to do it. The wisdom of St Ignatius is an extraordinary thing. In the seventeenth century, when the church was both in reform and counter-reform and was already being influenced by the hyperactive culture that was coming to birth at the Renaissance, Ignatius learns his way by having an *illness*. Having been a soldier and all the rest of it, he then has all this illness where he is forced to do nothing, and he calls his book – rather like a soldier would do – *Spiritual Exercises*. It looks at first sight as if it's another project where you could sort of tune up yourself and get cracking as a rather nice sort of bloke. But in actual fact it's rather purgative: the whole exercise for the month is to purge you of any idea about you going to *be* anything or *do* anything. It presents you at the end with a resolution – *the will of God for you*, that active, lively, pure-gold will of God, whether it is for marriage or secular life. Now, that was an amazing achievement and it's coming back, thank God. I hope it doesn't come back in the wrong form – I mean, psychologically to get people all engaged in some 'technique', which I don't think Ignatius wanted. He just put a guideline about reading the gospels for a month, and coming to a rather jejune conclusion in some ways. Because it's about embracing, passively – and actively – the will of God.

The theology of success and failure is such an interesting paradox. There is nothing in the Bible which would lead to an emphasis on success, and yet it has become such an influential ideology. Isn't it strange that in the Protestant tradition the theology of grace is preached by men and women who are frantic?

I find it extraordinary that what was a – I must say as a Catholic – *necessary* Reformation ended up with a tradition – it is now old enough to be a tradition – of hyper-activism, as if it all depended on *me*. I find this extraordinary.

It seems to happen in human history. It is as if there is something in the human condition which defeats even the central thrust of a new movement. Here is a tradition which is actually based on the theology of grace, and yet it becomes the biggest set-up of works and anxiety and frenetic activity that you'll find on the face of this earth.

You would have thought that, given a full-blown theology of grace from Luther and Calvin, if you're not careful, you could end up in quietism. And of course quietism was a phenomenon, a dangerous phenomenon, on the other side of things. But it hasn't done that. It has revved up. It has used – perversely, I think – the doctrine of grace to give you sufficient oomph to get on with a lot of activism!

And people then go out burdened ...

Yes, terrible. One of the dangers today is to take hold of that marvellous, fruitful image of the church as the Body of Christ, and then lay on every single person all the functions of the body. So they never attend to what Paul says about hearing and seeing and all that – so much so that even in the Catholic Church, which has a strong tradition about this, there are people who doubt whether the contemplative life of the eyes and hearing are anything to do with the body, so it's all hands and feet. Whereas I rarely hear them talk about the *diversity* of the gifts and functions of the body, so you don't lay on *everybody* the whole of Christ's mission. Is that right? If you listen to contemporary preaching, even when the substance of the preaching has got hold of a cardinal point about the existence of the person within community, you get the *whole* of the community's activity put on everybody. So they go out, Sunday after Sunday, with *another* load of responsibility. So the whole idea of the gift of sabbath and the grace and the rest of God are gone – within two paragraphs!

One of the things within the radical tradition with which I'm familiar is that people come along to church worried because their husband is beating them up, or they've had a hell of a week – and when they get to church the only thing they hear is about the problems in Nicaragua or somewhere, and they're made to feel guilty because they're not doing something about it.

The poor souls have to live with such generous passivity – you know, what they put up with – but when they come to church they're not told about this extraordinary thing that's enabling them to do that. They get another huge international problem put on their plates. This is where we come back to what you would say to the average minister or priest. Well, we get mixed up today about the difference between the pastoral work and the prophetic work of the ministry. Pastoral work can look like a very humdrum affair, though to the person with ears and eyes open, it is a most fascinating thing to be admitted into the privacy of people's burdens and joys and goodness knows what. But recently, both from the evangelical right and the radical left, there's been a pressure for pastors to be prophets and shout the odds about something. Do you know what I mean? Whereas if you look at the body of Christ, there were some apostles, some pastors, some teachers, some prophets – why should we *all* be prophets, or all be everything? Because the Lord will always look after the prophets – there will always be some lonely voice in the desert shouting for us to come out from where we are to where it's at. You know, the Lord doesn't leave himself without witness and prophecy. We don't need to bother about that. We don't need to have a little prophet in every single parish. And the average clergyman gets under the weather about that. He thinks he ought to be a little Helder Camara or somebody.

What about this business of prayers of intercession? Very often it's a matter of misinforming God about the state of the world, isn't it?

You know, I've sometimes sat at a liturgy where the intercessions are so broad and so enormous that God himself would feel the burden, and does, no doubt – that's his job. It's an appalling business, especially when they pray for *all* something or other. I notice this habit creeping in. I went into a church once and the minister said: 'Let us pray for *all* policemen'. I saw them as cops in New York, I saw them with helmets on in Britain, I saw them in shorts in Trinidad: my mind couldn't take it in. *All* policemen! I mean, I might know a bobby or two. But, if they ask me to pray for all policemen, I can't.

And if you weren't tired before you went into church, you certainly will be by the time you come out.

I test worship, communal worship, by one simple fact: do I come out lighter than before I went in, or do I come back more down, more burdened and more exhausted? Worship can *exhaust* you. Isn't it *fantastic* that worship should exhaust you! [*Roland collapses in laughter.*]

Maybe the instincts of the ordinary punter to be in his bed on Sunday are really quite healthy. Who needs to be drained?

Exactly. Now, when you hear these marvellous visions read during the course of worship of the lovely worship of heaven and the songs about the adoration of the Lamb, and then you think, my goodness me, if the energy exhaustion I get from half an hour in church is going on in heaven, then heaven's not a place I'm going to be anxious to go to! Is that right? It's not a love affair any longer. It's like paying your dues, it's like a back-breaking task instead of a love encounter. Now, there must be something *seriously* wrong. The minister needs to face this and say: 'Look, this is what I *know* it's about, and by God's help it's going to *be* about'. And therefore he or she is no longer going to go in as a miserable creature who's got to occupy God's attention for an hour, communally. It's got to be a *celebration* of the heart. And unless it's that, the people know it's not right. I think it's wonderful how people's loyalty comes uppermost, and they come. I find that very moving.

It's awesome. People go to church, even though they get all sorts of whiz-kids descending upon them and sending them out weary.

Terrible, terrible. Let me speak as a Catholic about that business of worship, because I almost feel an itch about what I've got to do for the rest of the few years left to me, here in Scotland. It's something like this. To my mind, the Catholic Church is not held together by the Pope, though he's a minister of the unity of it. It's not even held together by the Lord's mother, though again she's no doubt actively operative in what happens. It's held together by the sacrifice of the Mass. It means that, fundamentally, you can be, and should be, released from offering up worship that the Lord's going to say okay to. Because it's already been done, and Christ on that painful cross offered such a sacrifice which can be ours sacramentally as we offer the only thing we've got – and that's that dear Christ. That's liberating. It might be some low Mass gabbled by a priest who takes it on as routine, but the people know that what is going on is the perfect offering of the Son to the Father. Now, that's releasing. I think the Reformed tradition needs its own statement about this, because otherwise they're left with this Pelagian idea that they've got to get their worship together on their own, unrelated to this perfect offering, which is sacramentally re-presented so that we don't need to worry about all this – as if *we're* having to do it all …

As if God is up there at the end of each act of worship saying: 'I'll give it six out of ten for presentation'.

One of the burdens of the clergy is that often they can only arrange rather ropey worship because they haven't got many people. Say, in a downtown parish where the music isn't good or the organist isn't very bright, or perhaps non-existent, where everything about the service is all sort of tatty, in a tatty building with tatty people. It's a release to know that the perfect worship has already been offered finally and eternally forever.

And very often the ministers don't have much time to prepare worship because they're running around doing so many things.

Exactly. And on a Saturday night – I've been sometimes to stay in a manse or a vicarage – the poor soul has got an hour or two before going to bed to look through the stuff for the next day, knowing that it's going to be a pretty tatty performance.

I know that myself. I remember lying in my bath in Easterhouse on a Saturday night thinking: what am I going to do tomorrow?

It's really a terrible thing, and I don't know if lay people know the agonies of the Saturday night in manses. It's repeated all over Scotland. You can almost feel the anguish. Again it's about grace. The very worship is given to us as grace. We don't need to worry about all the terrible tattiness of our lives. God knows about it. He's taken it all on.

77

And the Saturday-night stuff isn't usually because ministers are lazy. It's because a great schedule of good works has been offered up. And by the time Saturday comes ...

They're exhausted, and faced with a Sunday performance which they know they're not ready for, and have guilt about it – though they shouldn't have – because the poor souls have been occupying their time with all this running around.

And afterwards, even if some generous soul says: 'That was very helpful', the minister knows deep down that it wasn't prepared adequately. He or she may be glad and relieved that somebody's been touched ...

... but the terrible knowledge that that little performance was all that could be put on is another burden which is unbearable. You could do it well once or twice a year, but you can't do it fifty-two Sundays of the year. And the guilt is uppermost at big festivals like Easter and Christmas. The clergy think: I must do something this year, and they get all sorts of ideas. But still it's not up to where they think it ought to be, and so it's a crushing burden – at Christmas!

Yes, and they've been preaching about the joy of it, while experiencing despair.

My heart goes out to them. I really am pained about this – the pain of the clergy. It's about the human condition. I used to think it was about the wrong idea of the ministry. But I can remember the day when I was preparing something about this subject and I realised, it isn't that; it's about the real human condition. Because God addresses us as we are, not in any *professional* way, not in any kind of specially Christian way. He addresses me as a *human being*. The very humanity that his Son took on for me. That's why I think this radical Nicene stuff about political involvement on behalf of the poor is also radical about worship and prayer. It's about *humanity*, not about Christianity. There's no word 'Christian' in the whole of that Nicene Creed. God was incarnate, he was made flesh of the Virgin, and he became man, not Christian. He became *man*. And if we spell that out at all the levels, we get into a kind of perspective that enables us to see the whole thing, not as a religion, but as a *new humanity*. It's about the restoration of man, not getting more Christians. It's radical stuff, that Nicene stuff. I would consider myself a Nicene radical!

Do you remember, Roland, how we students used to harass you at New College, asking you to justify your statement that your starting point for theology was the text: 'The Word became flesh and dwelt among us'?

The only relief from the terrible pain I used to experience when I heard that question came when someone told me that you lot also tormented every other lecturer with it. 'What's your starting point?' was a terrible question.

For us, I suppose, it was a bit of a theological game at the time. But actually, that's what we're talking about now – not so much the academic stuff, but the existential human starting point, for the church and the ministry. If you begin from the wrong starting point, you're going to end up with exhaustion or breakdown or despair, or go through the motions. There are a lot of people in manses who have only avoided breakdown by actually giving up.

From the inside, they've packed up. Outside, they can competently go on. That's a terrible state of affairs where the human being, in any job, can competently go on with something when their heart's dead. That's terrible.

And the vast majority of these ministers are not charlatans.

Not at all. Poor souls. Now, this business of the starting point. I would go so far as to say that unless you find a starting point, and it's the same as God's starting point, then you can go seriously wrong about the lot. I remember going to see the founder of the Little Brothers of Jesus, Father René Voillaume. This is very important in my life. In 1958, I was commissioned to do some work in Sheffield. I had nowhere to turn to except the continent. There was nothing that I could see in theological educational work in Britain that would help me to engage in what I had to do. So I went to France two or three times in the six months I had to prepare. I went to the Potigny seminary of the Mission de France where they were training up worker-priests. I asked Father Vanatier, the rector of the Seminary: 'When do you think a man's ready to engage in this kind of ministry existence? How long do you keep them?' 'Oh,' he said, 'anything up to ten years.' I said: 'When are they ready?' He replied: 'When they are prepared to fail'.

I went to see certain houses of the Little Brothers of Jesus. And they told me: 'Our founder, Father Voillaume, is coming to Britain in July'. So I fixed up to go and see him. You know, Christendom is a very funny thing. I passed the long grey wall of the Archbishop's Park at Lambeth, to cross the road to a mucky little cul-de-sac called Pratt Street. Number 7 was where he was going to be. It was on top of a greengrocer's shop, and the Little Sisters of Jesus – the French nuns who had just come – thought they would be pious enough to put their own little logo on the door. It was Jesus Caritas. And they put it in English. They put Jesus Love. Of course, it meant nothing to anyone. The only result of that was that they got a Littlewood's pools coupon through the door, addressed to J. Love Esq.! Well, I mounted the stairs and there was this huge man, with huge hands. And we talked about the business of the human condition and the gospel, and where the two touched, and how the Little Brothers of Jesus were setting on a pioneer course to find where 80 per cent of the human race are. At the end of it, he said: 'I'll give you a little word from Charles de Foucauld', which is strange coming from a pious man, a man brought up within the context of French Catholic piety at the end of the nineteenth century. He said this: 'It is more important to be human than to be religious'. Now, that is a fantastic statement from that kind of Catholic piety. And I took it on board. I thought: this is very, very much to do with the direction we should be thinking about. And it is this that really brought alive again the little phrase in the Nicene Creed, 'And was made man'. Now, that is an extraordinary statement, because it's non-religious. It's a faith statement.

It wasn't even 'and he became a priest'.

He didn't become a priest. There's nothing to give Jesus any status within the human race. He became man. And everything else that follows comes from that little root starting point – God's starting point, with the little conception in the Virgin's womb. It also interprets everything that follows, including the 'one holy Catholic and apostolic church'. It's subsumed under that great statement in the middle of the creed. So the radical Nicene position is really integral to the answer to all this hyperactiveness and stuff.

It's the starting point.

It is the starting point. So you were right, as codgers, to keep on asking and pressing the point: 'Where do we start from?' We did go along with Karl Barth in saying that the key is John's gospel, chapter 1, verse 14: 'And the Word was made flesh'. I mean, he was right. And however much I've had to sort of revise and be post-Barthian and all the rest of it, I don't think I would ever leave his starting point.

So what you're saying is that if you get that one wrong, you're off and running in the wrong direction. It was Dietrich Bonhoeffer who said: 'If you board the wrong train, it's no use running along the corridor in the other direction'.

Yes, there's disaster, disaster in your own personal life if you get it wrong, it seems to me. And I think it's meant like that, you mustn't get it wrong. I think there's a kind of inherent disaster thing built into it, to make quite sure that you do get the point.

Otherwise, it's like taking a message of freedom and ending up as a slave? It's like preaching a message of freedom, then you get to the end of your life and say: 'Why have I ended up with all this slavery and burden?'

The evangelising of the ministry is necessary before any evangelism is possible. You've got to get the evangel into the heart of the minister and the community, then something can happen. I think professionalism is the killer of a great deal of our Christian life, and in the ministry too. We see it in this idea that ministers have got to be competent professionals, equal in their status to an opposite number in the world.

And ministerial standards are very much taken from that, aren't they?

Very much so. And the expectations of success and worthiness are really coming in from the world. The clergy's loss of morale comes from this sort of worldly approximation of their job.

Well, it can only lead to despair.

It couldn't lead to anything else.

Despair – or people leaving, saying: 'If I'm going to do this stuff, I'm going to do the real thing and become a manager out there in the world'.

So they move over, and why not? Their family's better off and all the rest of it. Whereas even if you can get together some identity for yourself from those means, it's very hard to establish that identity within the culture you live in. It's not going to be given anyway, I don't think. The clergy will never be given by the world any pseudo-professionalism they like to get hold of.

That's right, it becomes really a bit sick.

Dear old Kenneth Carey, who was the Anglican Bishop of Edinburgh, and a great friend of mine – the reason why I'm here in Scotland, really – taught me one simple thing. He once told me, I'll never forget: 'The priesthood is nothing less than the consecration of your sheer, vulnerable and wounded humanity, because it's in that way that Christ became the High Priest of our profession'. I've never forgotten that. And he said that out of his woundedness, at a time when that was obvious. And out of that came that extraordinary insight, which I think is central to the real morale of the spirit of the clergy.

It's actually a very freeing notion, isn't it?

Yes, everything falls away, the whole world's hold on you. You can just shrug it off and laugh at it.

Because it removes the whole thing from the issue of status and professionalism ...

And career. Did I tell you about that hideous notice that's going up in some of those Anglican churches south of the Border? It says: 'Make the Church your Career'. I want to get some stickers and say: 'Come and get crucified!' Well, I mean, this is to go back decades. We've been trying to say the church isn't the clergy. The poster is assuming that the church *is* the clergy.

And it's a 'career' with a career structure.

How on earth a national church could sink to the depths of producing that officially, I can't understand. I really do get worried about that.

How is it possible to read the New Testament and talk about a 'career' in the church? How is it possible to read the New Testament and turn it all into a theology of works? And how is it possible to read it and turn it all into disembodied spirituality?

They really are damnable heresies.

And all the New Testament stuff is saying the opposite ...

The very opposite. Karl Barth talks about turning the rudder 180 degrees. He was talking about liberal Protestantism. But the job is yet to be done. 180 degrees: it's right round. And we've got to go upstream – none of this lazy, lackadaisical, downstream stuff which Newman saw 150 years ago.

It spiritualises everything into a kind of mush ...

Absolute mush. You can create clubs out of that, but you can't create the church out of that mush. And God keeps the ordinary bloke free of it. When we look at declining statistics about church membership, we could be looking at the wonderful work of God, of keeping people clear of the wrong directions!

So on the one hand you get mush and on the other hand you get drivenness?

Now, here is the point. For many people, the pulpit can be whip-and-carrot stuff. You move across from the damnation due to personal sins to a new whip, which is having to do something about every single thing that's happening from Afghanistan to Nicaragua. And there's another thing. Even the people who see the essential things that have to be said and lived can do it still with a hard dogmatic sense, if you know what I mean. The terror of the church and the promise of its never being overcome: these two things are always in scripture, in Israel, in Christ, in the church. Our real hope is in this marvellous seeming paradox that, on the one hand, the church is unprotected, open to all sorts of things, having enemies within and without – often good-intentioned, holy enemies – and yet it has, and thank God it has, the God-given promise that it won't be overcome. And you've got to keep these two things together: the ghastly perils, which would make us terribly paranoid if we only attended to that, and the promise that there is a little flock that will be given the kingdom. Funny sort of stuff, isn't it?

I was on Iona at Easter some time ago with a Jewish friend. He's an agnostic – Colin Legum, who used to write about South Africa for the Observer. *There was a bit in one newspaper about people in the Philippines who had got themselves crucified on Good Friday, in order to experience Easter. About twenty people did this – nails through the hands, and all that, with crowds of tourists watching. Another 500 people had themselves scourged with whips, some of which had glass embedded in them. And Colin Legum looked at this and he said: 'I thought you people believed that Christ died to stop all this nonsense'. It's like the whole works thing again, isn't it? Ministers preaching grades of salvation, and worrying themselves to a frazzle running around saving the world.*

And you can preach the crucifixion and think that it's a demand on you to afflict yourself with the most incredible, horrendous stuff. It's absolute perversion.

To use the actual Cross, which is supposed to liberate us from all that, as the means of actually doing it to yourself on Good Friday, is so bizarre.

It's incredible! O my godfathers! It illustrates the point that the whole thing is in danger all the time. I mean, utter danger left to itself, isn't it?

It's like reinventing the wheel, or reinventing the crucifixion. There are enough crucifixions going on without the church actually inventing more!

Good life! We've got the crucifixion visibly displayed every day on our television screens if we're sitting in comfort. We've got it right there. It's to this imperilled, almost humanly beleaguered people of God, a prey to all sorts of things, that this promise has been given, as to Israel. Okay, it will come right. It will not be overthrown. The gates of hell won't prevail. My godfathers, it's funny stuff! But if it wasn't like that, I wouldn't believe it. If it was a lovely, progressive sort of flag-waving triumphalism, and it wasn't this limping old dear, the bride of Christ, travelling through the desert with muck and stuff clinging to her, it wouldn't be *there*, it wouldn't be right. Part of our difficulty is that we still have this Constantinian idea of the church as a big power – you know, the European, Constantinian stuff which we've taken abroad and exported to other lands. It's still a bogey in our heads. We think we ought to be like that. And in some forms of mission, even in industrial mission, there is a wish to be where the decisions are made, influencing this and that, trying to get into the saddle again.

At its worst, it encourages the whole professionalism of the ministry, doesn't it?

Yes, you get in and you know about how trade unions work, and management and all the rest of it. And again, the little man, defenceless, is having to walk in to something that could do quite well without him, and in fact he's just an intrusion. That idea of being the intruder, the incompetent intruder, is a highly unpleasant one, isn't it? I feel that when I visit a hospital. There's this enormous machine, going absolutely beautifully, and you admire the marvellous competence of the nurses and everybody else, and you go in. You're holding up all the work anyway, and you can't look like the competent consultant in your miserable black suit and your dog collar. And you go in there and your only competence can be that possibly through your absolute ineptitude, the love of God might come through!

But you can't order that either. And thank God there are such things as the sacraments, which bring something to somebody which is not quite wholly dependent on the poor little personality.

I remember the first visit I made to a hospital as a student assistant. I had a long black coat – the kind the hippies used to wear in the sixties. I was at New College, and I was a student assistant at a local church. The place was boiling and my specs steamed up, and I sat at the bedside of this parishioner I didn't know. I had a conversation with him, with my specs still steamed up, and I never saw him yet! And then I bumbled my way out of the ward. What he must have thought of that visit! Imagine his wife coming in and asking: 'Have you had any visitors?', and the man saying: 'The assistant minister's been in'. 'And what did he say?' I remember Niebuhr writing in his journal that when he went into a big modern hospital, he felt like a witch-doctor.

Now exactly. That is absolutely true. I feel that especially when I go to the Royal Edinburgh, with all these high-flown psychiatrists and all the rest of it. And there's me going in, like a dinosaur, a cultural dinosaur, padding about. You're glad to get out of it.

There's a wonderful Glasgow folk song about a minister going to visit someone who is really ill. The minister sits at the bedside and can't understand why the patient is in such distress. The person eventually manages to write a desperate message – 'You're sitting on my breathing machine!' He's trying to help but is actually killing the man because he doesn't know the technology ...

[*The conversation ends with Roland helpless with laughter.*]

5

OPTION FOR THE POOR

Roland, the 'preferential option for the poor' has become a major issue for the church in recent years. How do you understand the relationship between faith, poverty and political action?

The problem from the point of view of the poor is that, along with your poverty, you are deprived of a voice. While the attempts to get articulation to the poor and from the poor have been very positive, some of the methods by which this has been done are ambivalent. Very often it is the middle-class white person who has been highly educated – and therefore not particularly deprived – who has been in the forefront of this process of articulation, being the kind of educator. I get letters from priests in South America who are obviously embarrassed by the fact that although they not only live *for* the poor, but *with* the poor – some of them have dedicated their lives to this – they feel themselves, as it were, 'needed' to help make people articulate. This makes their presence among the poor something less than a complete identification with the poor. Now of course, the second stage is much better when you have, among the articulate poor, natural leaders from their own group. The priest or teacher or what-have-you has to retire and sit listening, rather than talking. And that particular stage has been reached again and again, much to the discomfiture of the powerful, rich and authoritative men in government.

There is a sense in which we can – wrongfully, I think – follow the Marxist line in giving a kind of utopian vision to the poor, and not really heeding our Lord's realism when he said: 'The poor you will always have with you'. Christian realism doesn't allow us to espouse any utopia of any political form whatsoever. The hard, seemingly hard, criticism contained in Rome's reply to liberation theology – which, on the one hand, provided a lot of affirmation of liberation theology, but was in some ways very critical of the method and the seeming ideology behind it – wasn't wholly a reactionary attitude, even though that reply must have contained the opinion of certain reactionaries. It was really saying that certain truths of the gospel were being imperilled if you gave the poor the idea that a revolution, either peaceful or violent, would so improve their lot that they would never come to grief again.

Some aspects of liberation theology seem to run counter to the dogma of original sin in the first place, but also to the business of the realisation of the kingdom of God on earth, which is a *divine* action and not a human one. I think I have got to agree with that. We can now register the fear of powerful governments about this new phenomenon of the poor who know their plight and want to make it known, and have an organised web of interconnections with one another. It has a global feel now. The cry of the poor, whatever we're going to do about it, is being heard and must be heard. So this is a new factor which will never disappear.

One of the things that has changed the politics of the poor in recent years is the discovery of the corruption of the idealism of the Marxist state. It's been really corrupt – as bad as any sultan or anybody else you could think of. We have got to be very much aware of the fact that in politics, whoever gets into the driver's seat is immediately beset by all these temptations – making a pile out of it and all the rest. And this is just as true of the poor as of ourselves.

Sometimes you find that poor people who move upwards and get into positions of power are as ruthless as anyone else.

Yes, partly because of their insecurity. People who will be compassionately ruthless are the aristocrats, who never lose, and therefore they're nice and kind people, keeping their places. Whereas I fear the man who has come up from poverty, because he can be so keen on keeping his position, he'll do anything to do so.

Some of the most oppressive people are precisely from the ranks of the poor ...

We see this in the British bureaucracy. One of the curses of the growth of bureaucracy is that there is a new class of people controlling our lives, at the sharp end where we meet bureaucracy. These are little martinets who do little lowly paid jobs, but my word, they've got there and they're going to tell you!

There are people who would say that you shouldn't do anything about the plight of the poor because Jesus said the poor are blessed, and if they move out of poverty, they will lose their blessing. What would you say about that?

Jesus was talking about lowest strata, the *anawim*. In the Old Testament, there's a kind of tension between the righteous poor and the economically poor. I believe Christ was talking about the nobodies – that's what he really meant – they are blessed because they've got empty hands. They haven't got too much in their hands, and they can *receive* something. Whereas if you're cluttered up with everything else, even God himself can't put anything in your hand. So, he is saying: 'Blessed are those who are living so basically that they haven't got anything much over after they have eaten and slept and worked', and that if there's anything more it's got to come from outside. Whereas the people who live superfluous lives are people who are just stacking up stuff, and they haven't got any room. It isn't that God's against the rich. It's the rich man who has made himself impervious to being able to hear that there are gifts around. He's got the lot anyway.

Matthew changes it to 'poor in spirit'. The New Testament commentaries bore me because they do repeat one another in clichéd fashion, so that everyone gets a stock of answers as to why Matthew said 'poor in spirit', and we all trot it out. Christ must have said many beatitudes – he was always concerned with blessedness and happiness in people – so he might have said both for all we know. I think it is marvellous to know that included in the poor are the people, however well-heeled, who don't think much of themselves. I am glad it's there. I'm glad I can preach from that text as well as Luke's rather drastic, more stark one.

It's like being open-handed, even though you've got things?

That's right. You know, I think the present state of commentary stuff is parlous: this business of repetitive, rather superficial comment on the text. It's repeated again and again, and you can almost bet your bottom dollar that if you turned up a commentary on Matthew 5 you'd find it. It sounds learned.

Do you think the 'option for the poor' is a permanent shift in the church's thinking?

Church history is really the slow but inevitable breaking through – against all comers – of certain basic truths that couldn't have been obvious at the beginning. For example, take the whole business of the opening of the door to the Gentiles, which was the great crisis of all times. It meant that the Christian church didn't remain a Jewish sect. The church would have disappeared if Paul and Peter hadn't told of their experiences and got it through the Council of Jerusalem, which was the most important of all the councils. With the option for the poor, we are witnessing an enormous second great movement. It's of tremendous consequence, however much it is filled with rhetoric and hasn't been followed up. Just as the Gentile one wasn't followed up by all the churches at the time, so, in the same way, we're not all taking on the rhetoric or the declaration of the church today. But the option for the poor is the great second breakthrough to humanity. It wasn't on the plate when I was a Christian in my youth. It's a geological shift in the church's foundation, and it's of enormous consequence. They will date the twentieth century in time to come as one of the most important centuries of the church's history. And therefore when we get despairing, when we have our nose to the grindstone and all we can see is what's round us for a few miles, the great way of being joyful is to lift up our heads and see what is happening in some enormous millennial perspective, as God sees it.

How do you think that option for the poor should be exercised, bearing in mind the temptation to turn even that into yet another building of the kingdom?

The appalling danger of the new shift is that the 'success boys' will move in to create a kind of political, ecclesiastical power machine in which they've got places, and where it's going like a bomb, and write it all up in terms of human endeavour, and we're back to the same old thing – except it's couched in more deceptive gospel terms than the one before. Option for the poor, I think, means that we've got to have a faith programme in the sense that we are not only content, but happy and joyful to find ourselves among the insignificant – not only the insignificant people, but the insignificant actions, the insignificant things that we do and meet in the commonplace, ordinary, nothing-to-write-home-about situations. That's the real option for the poor, because that's where the poor have been ever since they lived in caves. If we don't see that, then the power of God will not be visible to us and we shall see our own power again: and we will have delivered *that* power, not God's power, to the poor. A terrible dilemma I see facing the churches is that we've got so many people who will come in on what is rightly called a bandwagon.

If the option for the poor is a geological shift in the foundation of the church, the task is to explore what it means to adapt to that as the will of God, rather than move in with slap-happy panaceas and what-have-you. And it means a conversion of each person who comes on to it. It really demands a conversion. Not only from the things we've done wrong in our implication in Constantinian religion, but a conversion of the whole perspective.

And isn't there also a temptation to almost glory in the theology of the poor, which is yet another turning of the thing on its head? Of actually glorying in failure ...

... so you're up to your eyes in glory for yourself because you're the biggest failure on earth and everybody knows it! And so it goes on, and it will always go on until the kingdom comes, literally comes, because it's the perennial temptation of the devil.

It's almost like wearing a T-shirt saying: 'God loves me because I'm a failure. Haven't I done well?'

Then there's the terrible judging of everybody else, the self-righteousness. I find this one of the most difficult things in my life: to avoid judging anybody who hasn't either seen the point, or done anything about it. That is the very opposite of what this is all about. There's a temptation nowadays to take the temperature, not of the piety of the person – putting the thermometer in their mouth to measure their personal commitment to Jesus, which most people fail anyway – but to find out how 'opted for the poor' they are, and deal with them accordingly.

This is one of the temptations facing groups like the Iona Community. There are certain radical code words. If someone throws in words about 'oppression' and 'solidarity' and so on, they're okay. But if someone talks about evangelical conversion, well, that's old hat. So you can develop a whole 'successful' theology of the poor with its own jargon.

Yes! You get the clichés coming out, and we judge one another by whether we use them or not. And that's how it will be to the end of time.

It's like the old class system, like an accent. Only with theology, it's certain vocabulary.

Yes, if the bloke's using it, we attend to him and treat him as if he's saying something very important. If he hasn't got the right words – just as they used to use the word 'blood' and stuff like that in the old evangelical business – if they haven't got the right words like 'oppression' and 'deprived' and 'marginalised', then they're out! I do love it! I think the Lord must be, at least sometimes, amused. I'm sure he is.

You have often said that the true hallmark of poverty is when you lose the ability to choose, you lose freedom. What has your social experience been, living in this Community, in terms of your economic or social standing? What observations do you have?

First of all, we had to face the definition we were given about what poverty was: this absence of choice, where inevitabilities determine the positions of all that the poor have got to look forward to. When we first started here, we had the usual itch to get somewhere which was ideal, and this was very difficult. On the one hand, there was a movement within the Community that said: 'We must declare ourselves to be contemplative and marginalised, and therefore we should be out in the country, rather than in a scruffy little mining village, to show people that we are removed from what is going on'. On the other hand, the momentum that was strongest was saying: 'No, not at all; we ought to get somewhere where it's obvious that to be contemplative in the twentieth century means to be in the midst of the desert, and therefore have the Community in the city'. We put the possibility of moving – which was limited, because we never had much money, so it wasn't anything we could do much about – to the abbot of Nunraw, and he replied that if we were thinking of moving, then we weren't poor. So it meant that we were literally tied to this place, by the fact that our economics prevented moving house, and because we interpret Christ's message to us to give up our goods to feed the poor.

So I think this is what we have learned: that we have to move into the psychology of poverty. Poverty isn't something you can profess and embrace immediately: it's one long, sometimes exciting, sometimes rather frustrating process of moving in to something, to a goal you will never attain. And of course we don't experience anything like the poverty of those who are on the lowest National Assistance today. What we do try and do is try and live within a social sphere. Well now, poverty as we have experienced it means that, in some ways, we have marginalised ourselves to even the norms of what people living at subsistence level manage. The last thing to go from among the poor is the television set! But it was the first thing to go here. I am still amazed at the number of people who can afford sets with some kind of help from the state; there are many people still, I've noticed round here, who have telephones – we don't. So in a sense we have over-marginalised ourselves from what would be the normal situation of people living on the breadline. [*Note: when the Community was founded in 1965, the bishop had insisted that a telephone be installed. It was found to be intrusive and inappropriate, and the bishop eventually agreed to its removal. A phone was installed in August 2003 for medical reasons.*]

The other thing is much more germane to the movement of poverty: we discovered something extraordinary about poverty. Poverty is really how people describe the Third World, not us in Britain. So we want another word. Poverty is the plight of the poor souls in the Third World, and we can't claim that. But what we find is that there's an interior movement towards living *in the present*, and being poor in that sense. We're not allowed – I suppose it's the rule most broken – to live in future projects, and what we might do, and what we're going to do. We are encouraged by the Rule of our community to live entirely in what's happening in the present moment, because of the poverty of the gospels that Christ puts before us when he says we should become like little children. A child is richly poor because he lives entirely in the present; he hasn't got any past to have nostalgia about or sentimental longings for or regrets about, and he certainly hasn't got a future, so is like an animal. A dog is exactly the same, entirely engrossed in what is there. It is this moment-by-moment quality that I think is the real discipline that comes out of not having money, or manpower, or the wherewithal to make a future. So your future has got to be entirely given: it can't be manipulated or controlled.

There is much more to it than keeping down the expense side. It's about the discipline of having the past and future taken away from you. And I think the whole business of the Christian gospel is this: forgiveness, and this 'let the dead bury their dead' business, absolves you from the past. You are freed from the past, to live in the present. I think this whole dependence on God as father, and whole business of sonship in Christ, is really all about not having a future that you can manage or want to manage.

And yet I think you would agree that the step into economic poverty was a sine qua non.

Oh yes. I am a Marxist in this sense: that I believe that the roots and stability of our spiritual life lie in the economic and physical surround. I don't believe it's possible to grow spirituality – this awful word – out of a comfortable assumption about economics which bears no relationship to the interior discipline. Without the economic framework, this community could only find a bogus way to spirituality – but I can't bear the word, because it's a word which immediately, when you say it, cuts it off from the roots and mud of our social existence.

It would have been something rather airy-fairy.

Absolutely. Like picked flowers. I think a great deal of this commercialised, pious literature is really about picked flowers that have been plucked from people who really did it, and offered to people in vases for their own cosmetic environment.

Now, what you have been doing here has been, and continues to be, prophetic, it seems to me, because of your witness. Now, let's take the television and the telephone. Doing without those two so-called basic essential commodities has been an act of prophecy, and – to use the Pope's phrase – a sign of contradiction, to the whole society, including the poor, who cling to these things. Now, it's saying something about convenience, and – as you also said – something about managing one's life, to be able to do without those things. It must have been a nuisance from time to time.

Oh, it's a thorough nuisance. For example, it means that you have very little subject for conversation. When Brother John was working at the works at Loanhead, as a basic labourer, almost all the possible link-up conversations were about what's on the telly – the fantasy world, and sometimes a world of information, which is accessible to the telly viewer and which is precluded to us. He found it incredibly embarrassing to say that he had not seen some documentary, or just some punch-up drama, which might have been highly useful to a conversation that would lead somewhere. Similarly, the telephone. You can see why it could be considered a necessity, because again and again we find ourselves cut off from the line of communication, which I must say frees us from a kind of class circle. If you don't have a telephone, very often the people who assume the existence of the telephone forget about you. They don't bother to use Her Majesty's mail; they haven't had any use for it for a generation now. So you just don't get in on that circle – which is a good thing in a way, because otherwise you can go on with a richness of contact, which we've certainly got, in the church and academic confreres passing through the house. We are rich.

Let's put it this way. There is one kind of richness you cannot get over, and it's one kind of richness that this kind of life needs. Now, this is a contradiction, because I believe that the people who would live this life are people who are rich in inner resources.

Yes. This is very much a Beatitudes theme.

Well now, this is a contradiction which, I think, we have to work out. For example, one of the disciplines we have is that in our conversation certainly, and in our availability to people, we've got to be very careful that we don't exhibit these resources in such a way that we are precluded from ordinary domestic and human conversation with the poor, the lonely, the unemployed, the people with nothing. And this sets up a kind of tension. For example: what you do with solitude is something you do with your inner resources on the one hand; and on the other hand, your availability to people who are inarticulate has to be preserved by making quite sure that you don't parade your ability to have thoughts, connections, quotations which could be difficult for people who find it hard to put anything into words. So there is this extraordinary thing, very hard to describe.

It's to do with superiority.

That's right. It's exactly that. And you see, in Britain, it's the hardest country in the world to do this, because your very speech cuts you off, if you're not careful. Yet any play-acting and charade of trying to be inarticulate among the inarticulate wouldn't pay off either. So in Britain it is terribly difficult to live this sort of style of life. There's a sense in which you're always tempted to be proud of the fact that you're going back to ... you can have a kind of arrogance.

Radical snobbery.

Yes, which one detects in groups that one has come across – and this is a constant danger, that you can make something of the nothingness that you've got!

These are all the twists and distortions that we place on the Beatitudes, but you've got this business of 'Blessed are the poor, for they shall inherit'. Now, it's always been very difficult for me, as a religious educator, to try and explain that word 'shall', because it's got to do with a future world, and yet it's also got to do with finding that richness in the present. What you've just said about finding richness within yourselves through the abandonment of all this stuff makes a great deal of sense to me, because it is about finding the kingdom here, and it's not a complete kingdom yet, is it?

No, but you've got enough of presage and premonition of the kingdom to keep you going. This is what the gospel is saying, and I sometimes think the gospel goes further than that. There's a way in which, I suppose, all the Beatitudes are present-and-future: all of them promise the future in some shape or form. All promise sonship and daughterhood under one father. All of this seems to invite us into an experiment as to whether the blessedness isn't already here – there's a present possibility of experimenting with the truth of these words. You don't go on in pure darkness, in the hopes that when you die there's pie in the sky. You get the beginnings of the kingdom – and I think the Christian experience will bear this out. The kingdom is already here, in the sense that we try to do the will of God. Yes, the kingdom comes when his will is done. On the other hand, the temptation is to twist all that round, to think that the great object of being poor is to get some of this blessing! Whereas I don't think that's true ...

We don't live as we would under conditions of the Third World. We get our inspiration from people who have left this country, and have gone and shared, without any superiority, in the actual lives of people in the Third World. This is where the life in the church is coming from. And ours is just a kind of spin-off, it seems to me, from what they're actually doing. So, when we talk about this, I'm not really talking about us; I mean we've made footsteps, centimetres in length, towards something that is the very vigour of a new gospel presentation of the Third World. We're only trying to live a parable of what is actually being done somewhere else. That's really important to say, otherwise this would be absurd, because there are high limitations to what you can do in this culture.

6

MOLE UNDER THE FENCE

Roland, when you converted to Roman Catholicism,
Professor Henry Chadwick described you as 'a mole under
the fence'. You obviously relish that description. Where
does this fit into this whole picture?

Well, this is a very interesting one. My decision to change
over the tracks to Roman Catholicism, in retrospect – and
only in retrospect because it certainly wasn't something
worked out cerebrally or even rationally – was a kind of 'gut'
thing. But looking back on it, it was really to assert, more
clearly than I could as an Anglican, that I really do believe
in the *visibility* of the church: that I believe that Rome is
right to be 'nuts on unity', as Owen Chadwick tells us. The
most dire thing you can do is to separate from your fellow
Christians; but unfortunately, historically, Rome appears
as if she is the obstacle to unity. Because her insistence
on unity is so great and goes into so many channels and
departments, it looks from outside – and perhaps for some
people from the inside – that her being nuts on unity has
prevented her from taking on the insights and 'yes-buts' of
other traditions. Now, in one way, she's opened the door
to being able to be more competent at that. We have to
remember that the Reformation was a trauma to her – a
traumatic experience that nobody who is not a Roman

Catholic can really experience, a fantastic wound to her identity and existence. And therefore she had 400 years of citadel convalescence. But now there's a tug-of-war going on within the church. I suppose it's probably always been like this, and it has its own analogies with things going on in the whole Christian world. Do you retreat into your identity fortress, or do you come out with the strength and faith to rely on the truth and reality of what you've got to state about central things? Do you come out and engage in fraternal and human relationships, where we can build up a place where we can talk about this unity that Rome defends, and I would say rightly so? It has something to do with her insistence on unity – or something to do with me, I think – that I felt that while other traditions may have unity as a kind of subsidiary, it's not seen as *part of the gospel*. The visible unity, the actual reality of unity, is going to be more and more necessary to state and to be, even in some deformed way. After all, Catholicism by its very nature is something that is dynamic – something you grow into. Even the Catholic Church would say that for individuals, the historically cultured and qualified forms of Catholicism have grown and are still slowly growing into the full measure of the stature of Christ.

Catholicism belongs first of all to Christ, and only then to his church, which *progresses* into Catholicism, as it does into holiness and to unity and to apostolicity. These marks of the church are dynamic, not things that are fixed. They're guaranteed in the sense that they're there as the marks of the people of God in their journey through history, but they're also *goals* to which all of us aspire. So, for me, the mole situation was about relating in my identity as a Christian to a church which, whether she likes it or not, is absolutely immersed in history, in global history. She can't get away from it. She can be stuck in the mud about it, but she's got to *be* there because she *is* there, in a way that other churches sometimes do not necessarily take on board. She *has* to take on the lot, and she's confused by it very often. It sets up tensions within her, in liberation theology for example. But she's *there*, and she never can be anywhere else. She can have all sorts of defensive reactions; historically, one can mark out places where she's retreated into some kind of hard-and-fast position which she clarifies and makes over-clear on certain issues, but at the end of the day she has to be in this turmoil, in the confusion of history, and she knows it. That's why I'm glad to be a mole under the fence – you know, going round the subterranean passages, which are enormously complex, and picking up bits and pieces, and digging a way through – some people say undermining! – the foundations.

It's still a mystery to a large number of people in Scotland, and England, as to why you took this step. Could you say a little bit about why that took place?

Yes. Well, I think you can only find out why you do things of that order after you've done them, in a funny sort of way. I don't think it would add up to much, if I put down – as I certainly didn't – a credit-and-debit balance of what Rome would mean against other things. I don't think I ever did this. It came from a decision of this Community, which we didn't know the full implications of. We had a review in 1977 or thereabouts, of where we'd got to ecumenically, because, after all, this is one of our strands, that we try to live in such a way that any Christian (and perhaps any non-Christian, but certainly any Christian) would at least find themselves beginning to be at home, and perhaps they might begin to wonder whether the labels that they were using on everybody were really very relevant. So denominationalism was at a very low ebb with us, and still is. I don't think we're going to be all that fussed about enquiring in the first half-hour of someone who's coming to stay with us or visit us, whether they're Catholic or Protestant or whatever they are! It seems to me that one of the things Christ was doing in the gospels was to show the utter futility of all these labels on people, like Samaritan, or Pharisee. He didn't label people. And this unlabelled existence, without any tickets for people as they come in, seems to me part of the gospel living. You discover the new humanity by being accepting of humanity, and not making partitions – and certainly not partitions within the Christian church – into a stumbling-block to acceptability.

So we didn't go into it like that, but what we said was this: if you live in Scotland, you're dealing with the underbelly of ecumenism if you haven't got a Catholic in the Community. Because nearly half the practical people who are doing anything about their religion are Catholic. So we said: what can we do about it? We can't do anything about it, we can only pray to God to open the door by sending us somebody who was a Catholic. So we started to pray for a Roman Catholic to come to this Community, so that we could display that we're not closed off. Well, we started, and then the most extraordinary thing happened. The Lord was answering this prayer, seemingly, not by getting anyone from outside, as the prayer meant, but by doing something extraordinary to me: not to my mind, not even to my heart, because I think that, like Newman, I have no relish for some of the outward phenomena of the Roman Catholic Church. [*Bursts into laughter at the very idea of it.*]

That's all futility, that's all the icing on the cake?
Yes, the phenomenon of the Roman Catholic Church – in its history, as in much of its 'White Man's' presentation today – being ruled mostly by the white man and by celibate priests is not a phenomenon that I think is clearly reflective of the kingdom of God. [*Bursts into laughter again.*]

So …
So, it was my guts.

It was your guts. Not mind, not heart, but guts.

Now, how did it work? Well, I found myself doing the most extraordinary things. Now, here's one. The first thing I found myself doing was not being able to cross out that extraordinary line in the Catholic diary. I always used a Catholic diary, because they have sensible saints' days all lined up, and Sundays of the year, so you knew where you were – and it was the cheapest one too. And it said in the front: 'I am a Catholic. In case of an accident, call a priest.' Well, up to then, I had always crossed out and altered it into this: 'I am a Christian. In case of an accident, call another one.' In 1979, for three years, I couldn't cross that out. It was extraordinary. I had a will to cross it out; I had a mind to cross it out, but I couldn't cross it out. Well, I was amused at this at first, and thinking: 'Well, if I go under a bus, some Irish priest will come out and anoint me, and I shall go up to heaven as a Catholic'. But that was a joke. The second thought was: 'That's strange. I must, somewhere in myself, want to die as a Catholic: and if I want to die as one, does it mean I ought to be living as one?' I wouldn't have thought too much about that, except it's strange that you are paralysed about crossing something out when you normally do so. But I found another thing happening. When I was travelling, instead of going, as I usually did, if I had an hour to wait between trains, to the Anglican church or cathedral, and pray, I found myself in York one day – again not knowing why, and certainly not as a voluntary action – in that cheeky (perhaps the most cheeky church in Christendom) church at the west end of the Minster, St Wilfred's. I thought to myself: what are you here for? Something – someone – myself – said: well, you're in here, so just say your prayers and go to the Minster afterwards. So I did. I did the same thing again at Berwick-on-Tweed, where I actually looked at one of those extraordinary maps in which you press a button and get a little light showing a church, in order to find where the Catholic church was. So

I found myself going towards there. And this after a habit of twenty-five years of going to the Anglican one.

Now, may I interrupt here, provocatively, and say that surely you had always been a Catholic? Why, suddenly, this use of the word 'Catholic' in such a particular way?

That is true. I once talked with Father Anthony Ross about this, and he said what you're saying. There is a sense in which the word 'Catholic' means that you belong not only mystically (whatever that means), but culturally, with the propensity of your thought and your intuitions. I had always been like that. There might have been a time in Cambridge where the pressure and enticements of a certain liberal Protestantism – no, I don't think I ever compromised with that – no, you're quite right, I'd always been a Catholic in that sense. What did Rome mean, then? Well, first of all, it meant a frightened horror that I was being drawn to something in such an irrational way that I wouldn't be able, either to myself or to anybody, to explain what was happening to me.

And that was worrying?

Very. *Very* worrying indeed. So worrying that I didn't say anything to my Community for two years; and it was only after that that I said to them: 'Look, something's going on in me, and I'm very anxious that you should not be too disturbed. Perhaps we ought to look back on it, perhaps this is an answer to what we're praying about.' And from the first, the Community – thank God – took it in that way. They didn't get disturbed at all, in fact very comforted. They said: 'Yes, I think that's the best way to look at it, especially as you're not doing anything towards it, it's just happening'.

So that went on, and I talked to Fr Jock Dalrymple, who was the Visitor of this community, and a Catholic priest, and I gave him a chance to make a remark. He said something that I think I would advise everybody to do, looking back on it. He said: 'Nobody on earth can help you about this. This is one thing no human person can help, because they're all in their little boxes and all talking from where they are, and it will just confuse you to go round asking advice from them and having long chats.' So I said: 'What do I do?' And he said: 'A very simple thing, but very frustrating because of the length of time involved. For one-and-a-half to two years, I would say a constant prayer: 'If this is of you, Lord, make it more and more urgent. Give the nudge a bit more strength to it. And if it isn't, then turn it off.' He said: 'I've never worried about what happens to that kind of prayer. God gives pretty good answers to that – sometimes he takes it away, and sometimes he doesn't.' So, he said it's quite safe. You don't need to worry, when you start praying, that you're going to end up as a Roman Catholic! Well, that was the wisest advice you could give to anyone, and I did this, and at the end I reported back that the prayer had been answered, and the nudge was definitely there. And with it came – well, a whisper, hardly audible, but looking back on it I think it was there: 'I will tell you why when you've got in'.

So I never knew any reason, except those two things. When I got permission from my own bishop to go and see Cardinal Gray, the cardinal was extraordinary, because I just told him those two things I've told you, and I said I can't tell you anything else. And he accepted that. I told him about the prayer, and the nudge, and everything, and he said: 'Yes. There's only one thing to do – go back to your Community, and ask them if they are prepared to take the pain of Christ into the very heart of their Community. I understand you are Eucharistically centred as a community'. I said we are, and he said: 'Right at the heart of your life will come a sword, and you will experience not just your own pain and the pain of other Christians, but the very pain of Christ, where his Eucharist is made an absurd division'. So I went back and asked them whether they'd be prepared, and I said we don't quite know what that means yet, so how can we say yes or no? But the Community said that this is part of a momentum, a vocation to live this, not only with some kind of purpose in things ecumenical, but just live it silently in a pain which will happen every day. And so we did.

Now, the curious thing was that, preparatory to going to see the cardinal, I was so unsure of what I was going to say and what he was going to say – and I was purely about the guts, and not the heart or the mind – that I said to God in a prayer, as I went towards the door of the cardinal's house: 'Lord, if he talks about your church, I shall know it's nothing to do with you. But if he talks about you, and your Son, then I shall know it is of you.' And that's what he talked about.

Now, that's the ground I stand on for my conversion; and it's nothing to do with some incredible intellectual, or even affective, musing of mine; though looking back on it, you can say there's a psychology to it. For example, it is quite clear to me that an old man, especially a celibate old man with no sons or daughters, needs Mother. There's no doubt that in the psychology of old men there's a sudden return to the need for Mother. And quite frankly, I have found to my delight that Rome, whatever else she's doing and claiming to be, is truly Mother Church in a way that I don't think other forms of British Christianity have been. I was also given the freedom to explore, and give effect to, and articulation to, my already developed Mariology. It was a great pleasure and freedom that I could now talk to my brothers and sisters in Christ with freedom about the Mother of God – which, well, one had always felt a certain hesitation about doing in other forms of Christianity.

Father Jock Dalrymple became the Visitor to this Community during the time when you were thinking about this?

Yes, before. One of the good things – to show that the momentum of the Community was towards having Catholic links – was that, on the departure of a good Church of Scotland minister who was appointed by the Scottish Churches' Council as Visitor, we put before the Council the possibility of Father Jock being the Visitor.

Do you think there was anything significant in that inspiration at that time? Linked to your search?

Oh, I think so. Looking back on it, obviously there was no intention at that time for any member of the Community to transfer ecclesiastical allegiance, but it was part of a movement which is still continuing, of discovering the necessity to live, and to worship, and to love, and to be available to people, on an entirely across-the-board ticket now, in a way which it was not before.

When you were praying for guidance about this matter, you said that you got a barely audible whisper which said: 'I will tell you why when you get in there'. And the why, possibly from what you've said since, might have something to do with the pain of Eucharistic fragmentation, happening here in this back garden, and also might have something to do with God pointing you, as an arrow, into the Roman Catholic community in Scotland.

Right …

… because your effect on them, and particularly on your fellow priests, has been a bit of an earthquake.

Well, I think I am a kind of maverick! They have to put up with someone who is coming in on most conversations very obliquely, with a theological training and background which is different from most; but I feel really rather moved by the fact that I am being used in a gentle but persistent way. I've got this Convocation thing coming up, where I am asked to give five talks on the whole business of faith and theology and sharing and priesthood, and that sort of thing. I am very humbled that I've been asked by the diocese to do that. But by and large, yes. Well, two things. First of all, Father Jock said: 'If you're becoming a Roman Catholic, then your scale of values, your timescale, has to change immediately. As an Anglican, you probably dealt with things ten years at a time, whereas in the Roman Church, 100 is called 'soon', and therefore a strange thing happens: nobody working for the good of Christ's church today will ever see the results of what he's doing. This leads to an enormous contemporary impatience in parts of the church, which is new. Up till Vatican II, everybody knew the score.

How do you relate, now, to your brother priests in the Roman Catholic Church?

Oh, this is a very funny one! You see, I'm neither fish nor good fresh herring in the structures of the Roman Catholic Church. I'm a monk, I suppose, in canon law. I'm a person who's taken private vows before his bishop. But I don't belong to an order that could ever belong to the Roman Catholic Church alone, because its very existence is an ecumenical monasticism. Therefore there's no church that can really take us in and put us within its own structures. Individually, of course, we are priests and laymen attached in obedience and jurisdiction and all the rest of it, to the church of our allegiance. I am, on the one hand, incorporated into the archdiocese of Edinburgh, and therefore in canon law I'm a secular priest; but on the other hand, from the point of view of my bishop – who has both received me into the Catholic Church and also ordained me, and put me here in Roslin – I'm still a marginal person, as regards the diocese. Yet I attend deanery meetings and all the rest of it. The second thing is that I'm retired, from the point of view of age. So here am I, not really categorised by the Roman Catholic Church. I'm an oddity.

A very puzzling person to many priests?

Very puzzling one. And you see, the temptation – both for the church and perhaps for me – is to wish to be recognised. Now, this would be fatal!

The wish to be accepted.

That's right. There's always this, within us all – both by the church itself, and by the individual: to be recognised, and be obviously ordered by canon law.

And yet I feel you have hinted, from time to time, that the hidden reason for your journey towards Rome was that it would have some kind of destination, some kind of result; that it would be, if you like, a 'postillion struck by lightning', that you would be in among your brother priests in the Roman Catholic Church, and there God would use you to do something for them and with them.

This is true. And you see, the very thing that makes it awkward from the point of view of canonical status is the very thing that helps me to do a little bit about being a person who can see a bit more of the game; so they use me, from time to time, to come in and say what it looks like from the line, as a kind of linesman rather than a player. And that's quite a useful function, to be able to do that. At one convocation of priests, when I'd only been a priest of the Catholic Church for five years, I was nearly the youngest priest there! I was trained, and all my training has been completely outside the Catholic seminary system. I was trained as an Anglican, for an Anglican priesthood, and yet they wanted to know how I saw the priesthood within the Catholic Church. Well, this is very encouraging, to know that anybody wants to hear what I've got to say. So I chose, as my subject, *communio*, because one of the things that I found, when I became a Catholic, is that although there's a tremendous lot of rhetoric, and although there's a tremendous liturgising of the fact of *communio*, and although all the main spiritualities are about this whole business of the reflection by the church of the union of diversity and unity in the Blessed Trinity, in actual fact the Roman Catholic Church, in its historical manifestation and in its recent history, has this extraordinary inability to practise *communio* between priest and layman, between priest and bishop, between bishops and Rome. There is this hierarchical, pyramidal stuff, which denies all that's now been affirmed in Vatican II, which still stands in the way of joyfully getting on with this associationism of the Blessed Trinity's life, and which is not about inequalities, and subordinations – it's the very reverse. Now, all this language of communication of the body of Christ, all this old and ever-new language about the fellowship and participation we have through the Spirit with the Father and the Son, applying to every baptised person – and therefore the consequences of all this in total openness and reception of one another's need for one another – all this is homework that the Roman Catholic Church still has to do. It is very conscious of that fact; but it still has to deal with a mentality trained up on this subordinational, pyramidal thing. Whereas the other way is of concentric circles of faithful witness and function within a total body, where every part is necessary and you've got to esteem and magnify the functions of the other because they're highly necessary to what you're doing.

What would you do to the hierarchy if you had the power?

[*Laughs*] Well, I would encourage them to go on with a movement which is already there. In the Third World, for example, we've got examples of bishops and archbishops who, first of all, give their lives for what they believe about the justice and the peace of the kingdom: where they live, in simplicity, the lives of the people they're living with: where their wooden pectoral cross is the sign of their wish to get out of the golden, bejewelled, hierarchic manifestation of power and dignity that the world, and the kings of this world, demonstrate. All this is happening. I would like to think that the bishops in the 'white' regions of the world would be able – and I believe are doing; I think there's an awful lot going on in this respect – to show that their way of life, their way of being with people, is demonstrating that authority in the church is not as the kings of the earth and those that rule over people in the world think, but this homely, dignified domestication of authority among the people. I think that's already going on in little waves. But I would like to encourage that.

Now, of course, Rome to you and me does not mean the monolith of the Vatican only; it also means people like Father Jock.

Exactly. Jock, for me, represented somebody who I realise would die for the faith. He had a kind of martyrdom angle to his life, which had to be lived out in the moderate comfort of British Christianity, but nevertheless it was there. I could do a little illustration of that, because it's very important. At the beginning of my rumbles-in-my-guts about Rome, on one extraordinary occasion the Episcopal Bishop of Edinburgh and Jock had been out at our community for the Feast of the Transfiguration. We were having lunch in the house with just these two and one or two others. After the rest of the guests had gone, a strange thing happened. The Bishop of Edinburgh – it was unlike him in a way, because he's usually very good-mannered – started on at Jock. He said, Jock, you don't *really* believe this and that specifically Catholic doctrines, and he pressed him and pressed him. 'Doesn't make any sense, how can an intelligent man,' etc. etc. And Jock quietly said, at the end of all this, which stopped the whole conversation: 'Well, I ought to be, and I think I'd like to be, prepared to die for it'. And there was a great hush in the room, and something happened to me.

I realised that there's something about the Catholic faith which produces a kind of martyrdom, a Thomas More situation. Now, admittedly, other people have died for Anglican beliefs, it's true; but, in the contemporary scene of late twentieth-century Anglicanism in Britain, it was not very obvious that there were many people who knew what they were prepared to die for. This was important to me, important because it linked up with my growing interest in what was happening in South America, where people were actually dying.

So, Jock knew what he would die for, and was able to defend it intelligently.

Yes, and this, looking back on it, was the beginning. This is where my guts started reacting.

So, an unexpected miracle was God answering that prayer by turning you around.

Yes. Another miracle, you see. They're all miracles. Because they're all impossibilities, looked at from the natural thing. I suppose, as I said before, from the psychological angle you can explain it; everything's got a psychological explanation, but it's not the final one.

I want to turn to a quite different topic, and a more outward one. How does it feel to be the age you are, and look back on decades of seeming immobility in the Cold War, and suddenly to have everything change so fast – such as Gorbachev saying to the Pope that freedom to practise their religion was a need for all people, and he was going to pass laws to enact this in the Soviet Union?

I find it absolutely beyond all thought that I've lived through a period where, first of all, the Roman Church itself gave no moral freedom to anybody to practise their religion unless it was the Catholic religion – which was changed 180 degrees at Vatican II, and without that change I couldn't be a Roman Catholic. That immobility changed in 1965. Then we were faced with the political immobility of the Communist states about religion. And I thought, well, we've seen one miracle of the Roman Church changing; not in my lifetime, if ever, shall we see a similar one happening. Then Gorbachev and the Pope. It was the change of another monolith, greeting the heir of a monolithic thing, and both of them agreeing on this incredible point which comes from the efforts of the Puritans in England! We've got to put this in its context, it seems to me, and it makes it even more exciting that the very thing that engages my attention as a member of this Community, as a priest of the Catholic Church, and as a human being, is the unity of mankind, signed and signalled and ministered to by the unity of the church. The curious paradox in God's great sense of humour is that he allows a toleration – not an indifference, but a toleration and a magnanimity – which originally grows from the gospels, is covered up for centuries by warring Christian vagabonds, appears as the main plank of schismatic sects, is transferred to America through the Pilgrim Fathers, and is now accepted by these enormous giants! I wonder if I can believe it.

At the same time, are you not worried at the direction Rome sometimes seems to be taking, with its Oath of Allegiance required of new deacons and Catholic lecturers?

Things now are happening politically, and socially, and I think spiritually, so fast, that Rome's perspective has got to be a bit more immediate than it has been up to now. But unfortunately, one of the Catholic Church's inherent things is to have delayed aftermaths of crises. In the Modernist crisis, one might say that Pius X basically was right, in that peasant intuition he had – to put his finger on something that was happening that would be the destruction of the faith; but he took out a great big mallet to kill a few flies, and thereafter left a kind of fear – which is still present in the central bureaucracy of Rome – of a kind of recrudescence of Modernism. And probably rightfully a bit apprehensive about a recrudescence of a new Americanismus, of a kind of permissibility stuff in morals and doctrines ...

... and individualism ...

... and all that, where the American way of life looks like overcoming the Catholic faith. So they've really done a pale spectre of the Modernist Oath again. Now, let it be said quite fairly: Vatican II has all the words of that Oath. It says they have got to give 'reverent and religious assent' to the ordinary magisterium. They're not going further, in the promise that they're requiring, than Vatican II documents. On the other hand, this rather negative way of proceeding is throwing up a kind of reaction they needn't have had, in certain people who are conscientiously finding themselves rather put into a corner, or they think they are. It's the psychology of it that I think is really – well, I would say reprehensible.

There is a danger of us having a Prague spring followed by a Roman winter.

That's right. And in a way, you see, we have this difficulty of relating this present papacy and what's happened under it to the other popes who were midwives to the Spring. [*This conversation was recorded before the death of Pope John Paul II.*] I mean, John Paul II is marvellous surely, and inspired, to pursue a great vision of humanity under his personalist philosophy. When he talks about humanity and the human race, he's as good as anybody; but unfortunately, if one may say so, he's also a Slav, a Pole, and he has endured, as we know, some of the more appalling enormities of the Communist oppression. So therefore, in the interior politics of the Roman Church, he has a bit of a citadel attitude which is not very coherent and doesn't easily relate to his other treatment of humanity and the theological consequences of the Incarnation.

You could say that, as a philosopher and a teacher, he has universal scope, but as a pastor he's still very much conditioned by his own local experience.

That's right. And I can understand that. And it's done a world of good in one way, because there was a kind of despair, and even the beginnings of a loss of nerve, under the later years of Paul VI. In a way, Paul VI's own nervousness transmitted itself to the church, and the church had to get back its nerve, and I think that was essential. And he's done it. But there is a sense in which, as we look on later, either he or some later leader will have to get away from this rather hard line of domestic ecclesiastical order. These two things are battling one another within the church today. We've got a bit of all this in each of us, and I think it is extraordinary that providence has provided us with a Slav Pope at this time. Before his election, nobody could foresee what he could do as a Slav Pope. I think it was providential that we had a Pope with a strong line, and who wasn't going to produce a kind of church neurosis, or prolong it, and he's certainly not done that. Therefore, whatever my strictures are about centralism and Roman curial fears and fantasies about liberation theology, especially about the freedom of theologians to pursue questions and unresolved bits and pieces – that to my mind is really rather serious ...

... but still the central thrust of authority was necessary and good?

Absolutely. I would back it up, and I'm very pleased it's happened, and I would take it as one of the signs that the papacy is an appointment by providence. Knowing that, we don't want to build into that some kind of apotheosis of papal authority: we want to avoid too much attention to a central figure that has to have our total loyalty in a sense that one can only give to God.

You have spoken before about authority in the church, and how these two forces of the individual conscience and the loyalty to the teaching authority of the church have to balance each other out in some way so as to produce an authority which leads by example, and service, as is happening in Latin America. So, we would hope that this debate that's going on in the Roman Catholic Church will balance itself out in that direction.

Yes. Obviously, given the human predicament in history and everything else, you're not going to see an ideal balance. It is always fraught with a precarious situation whereby you can only get as much right as you can, individually and corporately. Like the unity of the church, it isn't some kind of givenness that you don't have to attend to. Within the Catholic Church, we pray for unity at each Mass, and so it is within these seemingly disparate dimensions we have to pray and rely on the Holy Spirit of God to assist us in keeping a balance as much as we can historically. So it's not a terrible worry to me, but I'm very conscious of it all the time. I don't think the church will ever go on without internal problems, as if there's some kind of Platonic church that can land from heaven without any problems at all. We'll always have problems, good ones too.

A Dominican mentor of a friend of mine used to say that the proof that the Roman Catholic Church was the true Church was because it was the heir to Israel, and you knew it was the heir to Israel because it did exactly the same as Israel used to, by whoring after false gods.

Behind that tail-twisting remark is a great truth which I think we haven't really explored in some of our theologies. It seems to me that if we are going to take, as we are told by the fathers we should take, Israel as a type of the church, and her history, as St Paul says, being for us an example, we must unpack the adulteries of the Bride of Yahweh, as well as her dignity to be the Bride. And it is only because the Virgin Mary as the type of the church, the perfect bride, is at the heart of the church, that fundamentally the loyalty of the church is guaranteed through the loyalty of Mary; but it's not guaranteed by anything that we can get up to, as history proves. In some sense, the Catholic Church has been a very good antitype to the type: she has pursued all sorts of idols of power and dominion, In fact, one of the things that's happened – I would say the most incredible thing that's happening today – is this whole change of what is authority. 'The kings of this earth have authority and lord it over their people' ...

'... but this must not be the case among you.'

Yes. This text is absolutely coming in through official documents. The whole church has been put under some kind of discipline to unpack the rhetoric of Vatican II about authority in the church.

And this is happening?

Ooh yes, and it's inevitable, for all sorts of reasons. I've got no doubt where you've got to put your money – it's got to touch gospel support and foundation, and the powers of hell can't do anything about that. Of course, there will always be people who, at the level of parish priest or lay apostolate, will exercise dominion and be little Hitlers on their own patch. There will always be that, it's human sin, but the fundamental direction of the church's forward movement through the Holy Spirit is along the lines of the servant Christ. I would say that the evangelism of the church is going to depend on whether we can reach that point, commending ourselves through this particular back-ended approach to authority. Any other way won't serve the purposes of spreading the gospel.

What about the relationship between men and women in the church?

I feel here again, in retrospect, and only retrospectively – I don't think I ever thought about this – that there has to be a resolution of this upsurge of the psyche. It would need Jung to describe what is going on here at one level. But on the other level, I feel that the whole feminist thing is here to stay, and we're not going to get rid of it by ducking it. How shall I say this? I think that there is, and always has been, and can never be otherwise, a ministry of women, whether it's acknowledged, ordained or confirmed or anything, by any church. There's always a ministry of women, and there always has been and it's often been very much written off and canonically disregarded in all sorts of respects. As a Catholic, I would say that a resolution is much more likely to come healthily out of a Marian – of Mary – complementarity to Christ, than out of some secular, cultural affirmation of women in confrontation with men. The complementariness of women's ministry, which has historically been kicked about and kept down and used without acknowledgement, will come to pass. For example, we've got an icon in our little chapel which shows a woman wherever a priest is ministering. Now, I think it's along this line that a resolution is going to take place. It hasn't taken place yet in anything like a kind of visible and confirmatory form in the Catholic Church.

As Balthasar says, there are three icons of the church, and they're each of them essential. There is first of all the *Johannine* – the beloved disciple – as a type of the church, where the centrality of the loving relationship is established within the heart by the icon of the apostle John. There's the *Petrine* icon – the icon of Peter – who represents the structure and bones of the historical need of structure to pass through history – not as a boneless amoeba or some jellyfish affair, but some socially firmed-up visibility of structure of the ministry. But lastly and most importantly, the heart of it all, the chief icon of the church is the *Virgin mother*, whose ministry has yet to appear in one sense, although it has always been. It's always been there, it can't be otherwise – it's *given*. It's a datum. But the recognition – and the way in which it is related to structure – has still got to appear. They haven't been lined up in the way that Balthasar would suggest – though it seems to me that Mary, while she can be given all this sort of cultus which is non-biblical and non-traditional in a way, can become a kind of pious fancy, an idealism of femininity, and also sexually neutered. Now, you can use all this for psychological de-formation, on the one hand; but on the other hand, if the fruitfulness and the compassionate care and the whole business of Mary's real function can be highlighted and confirmed over against the matter of the structure of the ministry, then we've got a blessing. I felt Rome had all the bits of this, in order to counteract the worst of the confrontational stuff.

You mean ideology?

Yes, ending up with a kind of macho-feminism which would use the priesthood in order to confirm itself. Until we can be quite sure that the confrontational stuff isn't going to do, then the relationship of the structures and Mary becomes an uneasy place, which it still is within the church. Does that make sense? It seemed to me that in becoming a Catholic I was entering a field where I could explore all that without any kind of hold-up, and not thinking I was an Anglo-Catholic or a party man if I was doing this. I felt I had freedom within the bigger show to say all this and explore any amount of it. Yes, freedom, in a curious way.

When I became a Catholic, I also took on a rejection thing, which I'd never had before. I'd never in my life been rejected until I became a Catholic. I'd never experienced the rejection that blacks, homosexuals and women, I suppose, had known. I experienced it for the first time in my life when crowds of kids on a late-night bus from Edinburgh sang nice Orange songs because they knew I was on the front of the bus! I had never experienced that before, because as an Anglican I was given this marvellous flabby tolerance – 'poor old fool!' – but to have this wonderful feeling of being shoved out and marginalised in Scottish society by yobbery was a tremendous thing for me. I remember registering: 'I'm a black'. So the 'mole' experience is a very extraordinary one. You felt you were moving to the bottom of the pack in a funny sort of way, in spite of a church that has so much razzmatazz and power show. A curious mixture of moving into a church that always made itself obvious, and yet, on the other hand, somehow or other being kicked aside as something that's hated – not just disliked, but literally hated. It was a marvellously exhilarating experience, on the last bus from Edinburgh.

I remember Walter Fyfe, who was involved with community relations in Strathclyde, talking about a bus trip with Pakistani and Indian kids who were Rangers and Celtic supporters. Walter said that the kids were singing a really offensive Rangers song, the words of which were: 'I'd rather be a darkie than a Tim' – I'd rather be black than a Catholic! These Muslim kids were singing this at the top of their voices! Where do you go from there? It was absurd – they were insulting themselves.

Humanly speaking, there's nowhere you can go. This is where I think 'intelligent' Christianity isn't very good for people, because it doesn't deal with what *redemption* is about. Redemption is about the psyche – the two-thirds of us that we don't know about. That's what I'm worried about, how far that process is going on inside my tummy. In fact, the whole of my movement at present has been from head to heart to guts, in a funny sort of way.

As you get older in life, you realise how much the importance of the 'head stuff' is exaggerated.

And these other things are done down. Faith brings alive the heart and – slowly but surely – your guts. I find that the progress from head to heart to guts is my little thing. An extraordinary progression. And how much is due to age I don't know. There is a sense in which the age of a person matters, though I think the same thing can happen quickly to people. I've known people who've gone in three years through what other people take a long time to do.

And only come to what children understand anyway.

That's right, we're back to square one. That is really marvellous, isn't it?

Kids usually have this intuitive thing ...

That's right! And to have the freedom to bring alive, from one's own repressed childhood, your life as a child again, at the end of your life, is a marvellous thing. I find this so exciting.

And the intellectual part can be there to help sort out the other stuff, rather than tell the guts what life's all about.

Yes, that's right. In fact, it ought to receive a lot of its datum from below. But the intellect's a proud thing on the whole. It wants to dominate and give the orders. And the realisation of that is tremendous. As a Catholic, I've moved into a particular veneration of this extraordinary person, Thérèse of Lisieux. She only lived to be 24, but she focuses on the whole spirituality of childhood rather the mature, wise and steady looking of the old man. She takes very seriously the business about becoming a child and being prepared to be carried, and not always thinking you've got to walk bravely into it all. You might be *carried* into it. I find that really strong stuff, which requires a certain gutfulness to do. It's not an easy thing to allow yourself to return to simplicities because you think that's, well, a bit soft. I do think these three things of the Taizé prayer are important: 'May the

Lord keep us in the joy, the simplicity and the compassion of the holy Gospel'. Those three little things are the bottom line, I think.

7

THE SOUND OF SILENCE

I would like to ask you, Roland, about the importance of silence. Obviously, in your Community here, silence plays an important part – but what might it mean for 'ordinary people'?

Well now, when we started up here we didn't have a clue as to what we were going to do or how it was going to form itself as a community, and what were going to be the priorities. We were told by the abbot of Nunraw that we must leave the future entirely to what the Lord wanted to make of us, and we weren't to look over our shoulders to be like anybody else, and we weren't to think about numbers or productivity or anything of this kind, but just to simply live on the edge of the future, letting the future completely determine what we were going to be. But after about five or eight years of just working, living, doing what was asked of us, praying, hospitality, and various people coming and going, we found that there was a vision growing among us, that we were being asked to look at the gospels to ask: what are the main features of the life of Christ, his ministry?

We found, when we looked at it, that there were three aspects of our Lord's life, which I don't think I had taken on board as something to imitate or get into. First of all, there was this constant attention and bee-line that Christ made for the crowd. The crowd in St Mark's gospel is omnipresent, all the time. From the beginning of the ministry to the crucifixion, there was always the crowd. He makes a bee-line for them, and he is always bypassing the professionalism of looking after your own, in a rabbinic sense.

The second thing we noticed was that there was, at the same time, and for the same purpose, Christ forming the twelve. Perhaps more in St Luke's gospel than anywhere else, but certainly in all four gospels, there was this high attention to the training, teaching and strengthening of a small group of people who could sit round one table. The table stuff is all-important. A second tradition talks about the twelve as representing the twelve tribes of Israel. But I think the original intention of Christ was to create a group of men who could sit round one table to eat and talk. Table stuff was very important to Christ. He had a similar attitude to the crowd. He sat at tables with them. He sat at tables with his own disciples, and he made the table the pre-eminent symbol of his togetherness in the Last Supper.

Then there's this business of silence you were asking me about. We noticed, much more than we'd ever done before, Christ wanting to be alone with the disciples, away from the crowd. And also Christ himself going off without the twelve. This solitude stuff, the silence stuff, was very important. So we found ourselves creating a kind of silence in this funny old place here, because the house was here for two reasons. It was here for availability and hospitality, with an open door to anybody, a door from which we could go out and do various things in the human scene. But then we found ourselves, with the formation of our own community, having days when we wouldn't have guests, when we were alone together. We had weekends through the year when we gave special attention to our own community lest it should get frayed and lost in the bigger community. And then we found ourselves, after this period, building up an enclosure in the garden – where the huts and the brothers are – where there would be silence all day and all night, all through the year. There's a notice on the door saying: 'Silence, access only to the chapel'. So, a half of the place is given over to nothingness, as it were.

Silence is really a sacrament of two things. First of all, it's a sacrament of our own poverty. If you can talk – and even talk about your own poverty – you're filling it up with *some thing*. Whereas silence is an appalling thing, really. It means that you're facing audible nothingness, which in turn induces, if you practise it for a long time, a need to face the silences and the impotencies – where you're doing and saying nothing – which are really part of the human condition. You face a complete sort of poverty, a basic poverty, which in the end becomes a silence which is a sacrament of *death*, the silence of the grave. Now, this negative use, this negative sign of silence is something that by nature we duck. I mean, it's okay to go off with a book and, say, have a half an hour away from everybody and have silence, or to have the silence which enables you to sleep. But *this* kind of silence, when there is nothing and where books themselves take on a completely different aspect – because the book read in silence is *filling the silence* with something which seems worthwhile if it's the right kind of reading – at the end of the day, silence claims you, and you know that that book mustn't fill it. And when you get lower down, you find your desires – and even your spiritual desires and all sorts of funny things – are going on still, and they're rebuked and asked to come to nothing. So that you stand – well, ideally, one hopes to stand – before God, where his Word speaks most often in silence, where even the Bible words have to be listened to at a deeper level than the actual print, and where the meaning of the Word has to be absorbed in a kind of poverty which is reaching out for something to digest. So you're only too glad to do it, because you've got this inner and outer silence balancing one another, where the Word of God comes in to do the other thing about silence. And that is a sign of the *fullness* of God. We see God's weakness and his power. This is an extraordinary paradox: when he deals with us in human history, God has himself to come to nothing, in order to say anything. We don't hear from heaven – with the fullness of praise and thanksgiving and the saints and angels – a great Word which is bursting with exhortation and goodness-knows-what. God doesn't do that. He comes into the mess and the muddle, the incompetence and the death and the basics of human existence. If the incarnation is about anything, it's about this stripping, this God-stripping, as God faces his own Godforsakenness. There's all this extraordinary stuff at a deep level. Silence is the way in which God has expressed his fullness. And the best way he does it in revelation is by himself entering the silence of our incompetence and poverty, and showing the other side of the coin.

Now, there's another thing to silence, of course. There is the extraordinary ability of silence to open a door. Just as you have an availability door in the physical community life, so that place of silence out there gets full of people coming in to the silence, and you begin to see them in quite a different way. You see them as people claiming the space you've made, because they've got no space.

And a last point about silence which I think is very interesting. Living creatures of the vegetable and insect variety – I know this could be very sentimental, and sometimes is – become extremely important in silence. It's an extraordinary thing that they begin to have space to be noticed, and a spider or an earwig, or anything that's moving in one of those huts, becomes absolutely precious. You know you're sharing life with that *thing*, in a way that normally you wouldn't notice the blooming thing. I would go further, in my crazy way: I think I have communication with insects in silence. For example, there is a spider who is a terrible nuisance because he will come to where I'm sleeping at night and you sometimes have to brush him off. Well now, I tell that spider: 'that's your end', and I think he knows it now because he stays there. In other words, this empathy stuff reaches an intensity which is quite surprising. There are gifts in silence.

Now, what does it mean for the church? There's a whole generation of people to whom what we do in church is meaningless. We're filling the air with sound, and they don't discover anything to match to their own poverty. What they're looking for is something so stripped down that there's a nothingness, a consecrated nothingness, answering their meaning as nothingness. I believe the church has to get down to this level. As Taizé has discovered, where the song can cease and the silence is prolonged in a depth of prayer which absorbs all these bewildered, confused youngsters, they can sit there, then come out and say that what have they enjoyed most is the silence. Or again, we may look at the church that can read some incredible part of the gospel, and then stand up immediately and blurt the whole thing out with a hymn, making it impossible to reflect on what you've just heard – which is a Word of the incarnate Son of God!

'Fight the good fight' or something. 'Give it laldy!' as they say.

Or a huge great organ starts up and thought, prayer, everything goes, and you've got this 'church sound' round you. That's the first thing. Or, without any quiet time for reflection, the words of Christ are followed by a terrible man getting up and muddling it all up in his sermon! So either way, you've lost it.

When Taizé began in the 1960s, or before that, 1950s, it was quite a small community. I was out there, and the one thing I picked up was this incredible business of corporate silence after the Word had been read. I brought that back to our little Sheffield community, and we did it then, and we've done it ever since, and we're trying to get this over to a very wordy, noisy, organ-playing, ecclesiastical situation in Scotland. Silence is one of the most precious gifts we've got. Anybody who can't get it is a deprived person, and we're mostly living on our own self-induced deprivations.

One of the things I would like to see in the liturgy is five minutes' silence after the scripture readings – even if people fell asleep in it.

Let them have a little rest. Why not?

People would think something had gone wrong!

Yes, you've got to live through that initial process of embarrassment. And then, slowly, people would begin to appreciate that you're offering them a gift of God. I mean, if the Son of God needed those bits of solitude and silence, well damn it all, I should have thought his holy church would also need the same. But this reflective, absorbing, facing of one's poverty is very difficult. We're always shirking our basic poverty because we want to be *competent*. Even in prayer, we want a competence. The poverty of not being able to pray is not faced. Or if it's faced we try and buy a book about it or find somebody who's a guru or something. We cannot take on board that we cannot pray as we ought. That seems a very difficult thing for pious people to do.

Yes, you can get silence and then say: 'Right, I must build in silence in order to develop my spirituality'. It becomes yet another work.

You can use silence as a cosmetic for your soul and not see in it that God speaks most often in silence. Ignatius talks about 'the mysteries of silence': the Incarnation, the silence at the end of the Passion, Holy Saturday when nothing can go on – it's a prelude to Resurrection, the silence of the grave. And the actual facing of our own death and burial, and then at least a minimum of half an hour of silence in heaven. It's the *noise* of heaven that distracts me! I would like to know if I was going to have more than half an hour of eternity with a bit of silence! And if we believe in a space-making God, a God who is wholly other from everything he's made, then silence is a better symbol of it all than rowdy acclamation stuff. Is that right?

Yes. Continual racket.

And when you think of how much money in Scotland alone is spent on the refurbishing and buying of organs! I'd like somebody to make a statistical account of that alone. It would terrify us. We've chosen the most expensive musical machine to be the accompaniment of the praise of our poor God! So all power to those who take flutes and recorders into church, because it's the poverty of music that's going to impress and invite the new generation. This organ sound is completely outside their experience. It's the one instrument they never hear. Now, why should we impose an eighteenth-century habit of organ-building on a twenty-first-century church?

It can just become a religious instrument for a kind of club.

It's an extraordinary business. I mean, the Last Supper would have been drowned out of existence if they'd had an organ in the room! They sang a hymn, but they went towards Gethsemane with that hymn, and it was after it was all done. Sometimes hymns are used as wadding to fill up services ...

You can imagine Jesus saying at the Last Supper that he was going to die – and then Peter saying: 'Well, let's sing "Fight the good fight"'!

He was probably quite a good organ-player!

Yes. Pull out all the stops.

At the end of the day, our youngsters hear us whistling in the dark when we have these loud, rousing hymns. It's like Dad's Army! [*Wheezing laughter.*]

This is something we keep coming back to – the gospel talks about simplicity, and the church talks about power. And the question about how what's at the heart of it can still come through all that stuff in the church. One of the basic questions is how what you're doing here at Roslin can be incarnated by someone who's got a mortgage, with insecurity about their future and not a lot of time for all sorts of things. How do you translate this into that real world?

This is the perennial difficulty of church history. The church has always found it easy, like other religions, to manufacture a corporate expression of its religious life, in the sense that you can keep something going, from a religious point of view, as an exercise. Usually speaking, if you take the line of least resistance and don't think about the leaven and the light and the yeast of the gospel, you can be quite happy, following along a line that isn't very distinctive about the Christian faith, over against any other. They all demonstrate, in a sort of popular way, the congeniality of being together around a common belief. Christ doesn't spend all that much time kicking the institution. The synagogue and the temple were all regarded as something significant, his father's house. He's not going to take away certain traditional ladders, where people get up and do something. Sometimes they do marvellous things; in fact I'd never known a congregation, however sort of tatty it is, that doesn't have, in the heart of it, two or three people who are really doing the thing. And they've come to be doing the thing because they've been for a long time in that tatty affair. In the history of the church, there's a hidden history too – of a leavening, light, yeast thing where the small commitment of a little group slowly gets out and percolates into both the church and the world. And that's the history of the church, in a way – how the Holy Spirit's doing that all the time, with the most moth-eaten people. There is always almost a preservative, paradoxically, written into the institutional side by the commitment of a few. And it helps. The institution not only goes on by its own efforts to keep the thing on the road, but also because there are certain people there who make it worth while that the church should be there. And that's true also in the world, where the same people, or perhaps another kind of people with another kind of commitment, do the same for secular groups all round the world. I think Christ took this on board. He wasn't going to say I've come to abolish the synagogue. He's not kicking God's house. In fact, he commended a poor widow for giving everything to the blooming temple, which is very strange. I mean, in our radical moods we would think she was most misguided to do this!

Yes, saying she should have given it to Oxfam.

If we're going to be historical realists, we've got to take on board – as both Israel and the church have had to – a certain sort of structure that isn't obviously wholly meaningful, but which takes it down history, and doesn't rely just on the enthusiasms of the few. It's got a bit of historical bulk, as it were, which it needs – just as the yeast needs a lump to go into. So there's an ecclesiastical structural lump and there's a secular lump, where this yeast and stuff is going to get into. So there's that on the one side. On the other side, how do you get the monastic sort of thing, that's always teetering on a form of elitism and professionalism, into the 99 per cent of life? Haven't you rather cut yourself off by such a thing? By monastic I mean a coming away from the usual, doing the unusual, being a 1 per cent or looking like a 1 per cent alternative, seeming to remove yourself from what is actually *there*. It's fatal if that kind of concentration has no possibility of real contact with the real people who make up the church or the world. Mind you, contemplative enclosed orders can in some ways be closer to the world in its pain and anguish than some of the more optimistic rosy-spectacled active people who go in on their own ticket and don't really face the reality of the world, even though they're very much in it.

Now, the other thing is this: what are the basics that the concentrated lot are trying to indicate? They ought to be basics that are basic to the human existence, and not a special spiritual *game* they're up to. They ought to be plumbing down below the level of conscious activity and the general middle waveband of awareness, and getting down to the basics.

Now, the basics for those people, with a mortgage and whatnot, are things like anxiety – things to do with being overwhelmed, pressured. All these things belong to a basic human condition of life in its complexity, and seem to be out of range of the simplicity of the concentrated lot. In actual fact, the main purpose of the concentration and simplicity of the concentrated group is the conscientisation of human existence – not spiritual existence, but *human* existence. When everything is stripped away, we still remain frightened about health, and death, and not being able to cope. So when people come to you, they should be able to discover a place where all the top surface stuff about their lives, their top surface worries, are put aside, and you can start saying: 'What's the basic thing, what's really biting you?' Down in your human existence, you've been born into this world with things that you share with African people, I mean people who don't even know where the next meal's coming from. They're sharing with us something very basic, and we never discover it because we cover it up with thinking we can cope. So, this simplicity of life ought to be revealing. If it isn't, it's failing because it's doing something as a little spiritual exercise. It's a selfish little nonsense, and God will disregard it unless it's made available to let people become aware of the basic poverty of all our lives. It doesn't matter how well-heeled a person is, he or she needs to be faced with what is a fact. And then the reality that they face is something God can deal with. God can't deal with our unrealities. That's why lying and self-deceit and illusion are so bad and destructive to us all, because he can't deal with them until we've discovered them. And consequently, I would say to anybody – and this goes for people in churches – they need constant assessment. Any business would have an assessment of what is going on. I find it extraordinary that people can go on with programmes of church life without a radical assessment. Are we doing what we should be doing, and on what basis do we do it? What are our assumptions?

Certainly, monastic life and alternative society life in the Christian church needs constant assessment. I would say that, once a year, you need to ask: 'What are we up to? Do we need to be doing it? And who's listening?' And not judging it by numbers and all that – but are we really in touch with the real? And by the real, we're talking about the poor old dears, and the newly married people with the mortgages. Are we really able to say to them: 'Well now, that's where *you* are. It looks so far from where *we* are, but in actual fact, part of the things you're distressed about, and what we're trying to discover, is the *human* thing'? Because that's what's been redeemed, not some blooming religious light that's been raised up. You don't need to die on a cross to get some more religion going! You can die in your bed with the 'flu, can't you, or I mean, you could have a marvellous funeral. But if you want to really buy back into the human condition, then death's your only way. You need to take that simple fact on board. Isn't that right? In the same way, just because Christ's life ends up in a way that *we* don't expect to – or we hope not to – on a kind of dust-heap of humanity, it's highly relevant to all the intermediate stages of our living. Because if he hadn't done the drastic, he couldn't have done the lot. It's this yeast stuff, losing itself and all that. Somebody's got to do an *extraordinary* thing in order to get at the *ordinary*. It's a paradox.

It's on the edge?

That's right. Otherwise we could become unconscious of the edge of the gospel, if everybody was called to just do what the 99 per cent do. You always need the 1 per cent of people who are called to stand outside, to be radical to the rest. If they were all on the same ticket, engaged in the form of life that they took up in their family, or class, or education, then there would be something missing. You see, there's Saint John the Baptist. He's an oddity, isn't he? He's outside the blooming lot, church and state, and a worry to his clergyman father. I mean, what did he become? They had all that marvellous 'do' at his birth and the tremendous great religious affair in the temple. They must have had the pious people around the house for the birth of the son – and then he does all this crazy stuff. Why do we have all these funny oddities? I mean, most of the Bible is written by people who removed themselves from a lot of it, didn't they? So, when they talk about the *prophetic* aspect of monasticism, as the original ones did, they're talking about an element that the church has always sort of pushed up somewhere.

I would say that the Iona Community is a threat – the unusual is always a threat to the usual – because it is a form of recovery of the community tradition within the church. This was a threat to those who thought themselves put down by people with a commitment which was going as far as economic commitment and all that stuff. This is a threat to the usual, but it is needed. And I would hope that, just as with Taizé, Protestant Scotland would develop its own form of monasticism and celibacy, because that's an element which is in the New Testament – and we've got a saviour who was one of them anyway! It's curious that there's been a kind of cover-up of all that since the Reformation.

And it all becomes very kind of normal ...

Yes, the thing that would put us to sleep. These are all jabs to the people who are looking at it, jabs to keep us awake and alert.

The Reformation itself was a very radical movement, yet it's interesting that within a few generations it had itself become institutionalised. And, like the Iona Community, you have to say to yourself: why are we doing this?

That's right, but this is the nemesis of all these things. Somehow or other, they cannot be guaranteed a second wind. I remember Father Kelly, the Anglican founder of the Society of the Sacred Mission, saying to me that he thought every community ought to reform on the death of its founder, because it was impossible to go on anybody else's energy. Just as the Iona Community has to ask: what's happening now? What energy, what vision now?

Most leaders of the Community fear – because they know the Community cannot go on forever – that they might be the one who puts it onto the rocks. In fact, that's maybe what should happen some time in the future.

And one of the things we have to do in our little show here in Roslin is to answer one very serious question at our annual general meeting: does God want us to go on? Why should we assume he does?

Just as in the Iona Community: why are we doing this? Are we doing it because George MacLeod did it, or are we doing it because George didn't do it?

These are quite basic questions. I think communities are absolutely under the necessity of radical yearly assessment.

Communities don't have the same grinding thing that the church has, you know, of year in, year out, for ever and ever, amen.

There's nothing more useless than the bit of yeast that isn't doing its work. The gospel's full of the uselessness of the gadfly that ceases to gad. A creature like that is non-functional. I'd rather be a heavy old elephant than that.

No *raison d'être* at all. Now, this is very important, I think, when it comes to examining the relationship between the 1 per cent group, the ginger group as it were, and the rest. Because it can pack up quite easily when it's not really being effective. You're doing something because you're driven from behind. To my mind, the true reformation would have come if they had seen behind the decrepit and badly administered and tyrannical monastic traditions of Scotland, which were certainly there. The religious orders were in a terrible mess. But instead of reforming them, they abolished them. They couldn't see the point of any of it. One can understand historically why not, but it's a pity that over 400 years they've been so slow to take on ... well, Taizé's a breakthrough, because *there's* a Protestant community, lighting a beacon in Europe. We're beginning, in Scotland, to warm one or two hands by that fire. And there has always been that consecrated order of deaconesses – marvellous, a lovely lot. In fact, I would say that deaconesses and the Woman's Guild keep the Church of Scotland going!

I agree. That's where the most radical thinking in the Church of Scotland is coming from. All the action about AIDS – it's not coming from middle-class men but from the much-maligned Woman's Guild.

I know, it's marvellous. That's true of Scotland, more than anywhere else I think. I remember someone saying to me: Never despise an invitation to talk to the Woman's Guild. It has its own formalism, but you'll find more people there who are ready to go places than in the kirk session.

Maybe it's because they've been running homes, and wiping backsides and all that.

As a Catholic, I would say they're upholding the whole thing, the Marian ministry – which was a ministry to Christ. It's pretty high ministry that, eh?

And it's being done very unobtrusively.

Like Mary and the nobodies. The men always have this extraordinary idea of being part of something that's obviously *viable*. Like the disciples. Think of the Passion. That's the last place where chief places matter, yet they're still talking about who's going to be what. A chair next to Christ with three people trying to sit on it!

8

THE SPIRIT AND THE FLESH

Roland, what do you make of the current vogue for 'spirituality'?

As we all know, the 1960s produced a desire for the guru, and a generation went to Kathmandu and further afield to find their gurus. In the 1970s, this guru idea came into the Christian church. You had to have not only a communal, corporate belonging to a church – which might have been a sort of club existence, a religious club with a denominational tag – but the high-flyers had to have some sort of guru man or woman who was the great guide into the promised land of the spirit. So much so that I would say that, of the requests to go and speak to people, eight out of ten of the subjects given me are about what they call 'spirituality'.

Now, 'spirituality' is a hideous word, because it's one more step towards the bloodletting of the faith, if it's taken – as it usually is – as some extraordinary elitist 'extra', or even elitist necessary component to reaching heaven and God-acceptance. It ploughs into the 'good works' syndrome because it now produces good works and what you're going to do with your lovely spirit and soul – brushing it up and giving it exercises and all the rest of it. It also introduces the idea that the Holy Spirit is about something that releases us from our bodily existence. Now, this is not true of *all* things that call themselves spirituality, because obviously, under this ticket, there is a great deal of faithful pinning down to actuality of the person, the family, society and political involvement. And there is many a priest and many a minister and many a good soul who will cheerfully go talking about spirituality without questioning the word, and just using it to get over the right sort of things.

But I think the word itself has to be expunged from our Christian language because of what has happened to it, by and large, and we've got to make quite sure that we know that it really isn't a word that has a very long history. It was popular in the seventeenth-century French devotional books, and it's got the anaemic sound in French of *spiritualité* – the bloodless possibility of thinking of our relationship with God as part of our lives called 'religion'. Well now, so far as I know, the only way we can counter this, and the way I try to do it, is to say: 'I won't talk about spirituality. I've got a better word, because it's in the Bible and it's in the tradition and it's absolutely rooted in the faith – and that is the word "embodiment".' Because I believe absolutely that wherever the Holy Spirit is, there is always embodiment. There's the embodiment of Israel, and the prophetic gift of the Spirit to get the noses of the nation – priests and king and people – against the reality of the Law's embodiment in life, in family and in society, with all the demands that are made on us, the actual physical existence and quality of our life. More important, there's the overshadowing of the Spirit in the Blessed Mary's conception, which is the beginning, as the collect says, of our salvation. This embodiment of Christ within the womb of Mary is the work of the overshadowing spirit, just as the initial work of the overshadowing spirit is chaos – the embodiment in form and shape of the physical universe. Then again, at Pentecost, which is really a corresponding annunciation event, there was the conception and birth of the embodiment of the Christian society, which Paul rightly calls the body of Christ – the embodiment of Christ in his society where he, in his embodied, risen state is still the head, and is not identified completely with his ecclesial body. And in the life of that embodiment there is the embodiment of Christ in his gift of himself to us and through us to others in the holy sacrament. This is something that we've got to think through and, by dialogue with each other across the traditions, find some way of stating what must be a common faith: namely that the sacrament, if it is to be the central worship of the church, must in some real way reflect and guarantee to us the embodiment of Christ among his people.

And lastly, of course, is the embodiment of Christ *in the poor*. It's all very well to ecclesiasticise the real presence, so that we have the 'religious' real presence in a eucharistic rite and in the ecclesial community; but if we neglect the real presence of Christ in the poor – which is the very basis of our last judgement – then we can make even the embodiment of Christ in church and sacrament into a 'spirituality' – even though it's about *embodiment*. It hasn't reached its term unless we see it coming to us in the distress of people in their *bodily* existence, and in society: the aches and pains and grievous violences and degradations, and all that. I think this is probably the most important ecumenical problem. If ecumenism doesn't major on our reflection on the embodiment of the Spirit, as the gift of the Father through Christ, then I think we can waste our time. Ecumenical progress, I think, can be measured by whether we're getting nearer to or further away from this great issue, because it's the issue of all Christendom: after the demise of Marxism in Europe, how are we going to fill the vacuum of faith? That is the great question for the European churches. The whole business is about embodiment because the success of Marxism – though it wasn't as long as some of us fancied – lay in the fact that Marx could stand Hegel on his head and *embody* German idealism, to give a faith, a secular faith, for a society. In the vacuum caused by all that's gone on in Europe, it's now *of necessity* to be ecumenical, and global about our presentation of the faith as embodiment of the love of God in Christ, in the church and in the poor. Ecumenism is no luxury or some professional little ploy for one or two people at the top of things.

If the whole thing moves on to a very ethereal spirituality, then you've lost the game, haven't you?

We've lost the game, we've gone into Platonism, and we've got no answer, it seems to me, to the Don Cupitts of this world. There's no answer to the Feuerbachian revival of aspirational humanism.

And if spirituality then becomes linked to capitalism, if it is disembodied, and torn out of its incarnational context ...

... it gets embodied in secularisation of a demonic kind, if you're not careful. There's a sense in which it is impossible for the human being to be content with a kind of disembodiment. Whatever we mean by the resurrection of the body, we're talking about something about a human being's impossibility of thinking in terms of *pure spirit*. Whatever we say about ourselves, we are embodied in society. So, if you don't get the right embodiment which is given to us in the revelation, you get the unaware embodiment of all this in demonic structures.

Yes, you get plenty of embodiment there.

It will embody itself, but it won't be the holy body of Christ. This is what we've got to say.

George MacLeod saw all this in the 1930s, didn't he?

Yes. To see that all these years ago needed the prophetic gift, because it was certainly opaque to all of us.

It's interesting that, at the time when George MacLeod was being demonised in the church as a Communist,

*he was actually saying Communism is finished. It's
all documented. The church had a big commission
on Communism, and George was saying: 'If the
church thinks that people are going to turn away from
Communism to Christianity, they've got another think
coming, because the people are not going to be impressed'.
He was really saying that, unless there's an embodied
alternative, they won't take it on.*

It's absolutely true to this day, and whether we've got
ourselves ready for this crisis is very doubtful.

*I think that in Scotland, which has got at least some of the
East European dimensions about it, people like George
MacLeod and Geoff Shaw and yourselves are resources
for people who are trying to rethink these things. People
are coming at it from different directions, but they're
agreed that unless it's an embodied thing, forget it. If it
isn't, the future is going to be ethereal garbage linked to
multinational capitalism.*

This is the gravest danger, I would say, since Gnosticism. It's
the gravest danger to the church at present. Disembodiment
really is a form of Gnosticism. The Gnostics wanted to get
rid of the 'body' stuff in the faith. It's very interesting that
we've got a Gnostic crisis coming on us. It's already here.

Now, one more point about this. Ecumenism can be
thought of as a kind of peripheral extra activity. And for
most congregations I suppose it is. I mean, we give a little
nod occasionally, with the Church Unity octaves, and the
exchange of pulpits, and being nice to one another, and all
the rest of it. Now, the reason why ecumenism has become a
kind of hobby for the few, and its pace is not all that swift, is
because, it seems to me, we've still got a kind of 'spirituality'
stuff about the church. The embodiment of the faith means
a visible expression of that embodiment, not a 'spiritual
unity'. The world would never believe in the 'spiritual'
unity of the church, because they can't *see* spiritual unity. I

wonder if *we* can. It's only real when it's embodied, when I'm with people because I know Christ has got us together, and it's not a bit of idealism that we should be together. We are together in the real ontology of the church – visibly together, bodily. Now, I find in Scotland that it's almost impossible to register how far Scottish Christianity has taken on board true *embodied ecumenism*. It has almost got into this rut of 'We're all spiritually kind and nice to one another, we are tolerant, we are decent. We no more light bonfires and call one another names, and that's all we need to do.' I think that, if that view wins, we're failing in this enormous business of providing Europe with an embodied presentation of a faith that can treat people where they are in society, as persons and nations, as embodied. And, unless we can do that as an embodied people, it's no use. I think we've got to change our tune about ecumenism. We've got to really think this one out. And when we come together, it's got to be in the sense that we're not just going to create ourselves, as a work, but we've already been *given* it in Christ. We've got to make quite sure we *receive* this gift of embodiment. It's not work we've got to do; we've got to say: 'We've got it. How do we express it?'

I used to find that in Easterhouse this embodiment business was so important because talk about unity didn't cut any ice with anybody. I mean, who was interested? Nobody. It was an ethereal notion.

Absolutely. You'd have to be a trained minister to be interested at all.

What was very easily understood was Protestants and Catholics actually working together, visibly. That was the only thing that mattered.

I think that ecumenism really wants to look at where we can be at our best hour. That is to say, where we are embodied and can be *seen to be* embodied – and we are already being able to see all that when we are attending together to the needs of humanity. And wherever that goes on, the world is seeing something. The sacramental and faith commitment embodied in one obviously united fellowship will only emerge when we've embodied ourselves in care for the world. It's that one that we should start with: and slowly the prayer, the Bible-reading, the sacraments and all the rest will fall into place. God is not going to allow us to have a 'religious' embodiment without this one.

Some 'nice' notion of spirituality or 'it's nice to be nice' won't do, will it? Paganism has got a lot more integrity than that stuff.

Absolutely. And I think we've got to work away at this so that it's based upon the embodiment that Christ himself wills as he makes his option for the poor, and says that the rich are in danger of losing out on the whole thing. We've got to take all that so seriously that we are together on this option. And where that happens, the world crumbles before it – and they will kill us. That is where the pain is going to come for us, together. It's only when pain and persecution and being shoved to the margin with the poor is the embodiment of us all, together, that Christ can give us the graces of union and sacrament and faith. There's a highly important theological engagement going on just now, needing quite prophetic and shrewd minds – which we're not very abundantly blessed with. I've noticed that, in the Catholic world and the Protestant world and the Orthodox world, the theologians are attempting, at almost the eleventh hour, to find the target centre of faith, so that the complexities of dogmatic theology, as it has come to us through tradition, are overcome by centring on the unique features of the faith. And the unique features of Christian faith are the Blessed Trinity and the Crucifixion. Once you've talked to Jew or Muslim or Buddhist or whatever, you notice, sooner or later, that you're laying the groundwork of friendship and common stuff, in order that one day you're going to be able to talk about the two crucial elements of the Christian faith which don't exist in any other. This whole business of comparative religion has to be carefully handled, so that you know what you're doing. You are laying this groundwork of common affirmations and similarities, but at the end of the day, unless the Christian is there to say what is unique to his faith – not through any merit of his – then he's losing out and coming into a relativism which is going to defeat the faith of our children, if we're not careful.

Now, in order to do this, the theologians are concentrating on the corporate, communal, personal, eternal life of the Godhead in Blessed Trinity – a trinity of love-bonding. We know this through the crucifixion of the Son of God which itself is the embodiment into our condition at its worst and most hideous, and of the love that can overcome the whole of this. So, these two unique things are being set, by the best of our theologians, as the real centrepiece around which the hierarchy of truths we're talking about find their place. Ecumenically, this is important because we're now stressing, rather rhetorically and not really thought out yet, our common baptism – which is again into those two things, the Trinity and the death and resurrection of Jesus Christ, the central points. Ecumenically, we're going to have to spell this out and live it. Live it, not just talk about it.

Now, it seems to me that on the one hand you've got that emphasis, and on the other hand you've got this prophetic stress on embodiment. The love of God will not be presented to anybody – even to ourselves, let us face it – unless it's embodied. Is that right? So, I see all this as the big movement of genuine theology. If these things aren't present when I read something, I find myself asking: 'Why am I not interested in this book? It's shrewd, it's got cunning, it's clever. Academically it will pass, but it doesn't grip.' Why? Because it is not centred on the central things we've been talking about.

The other point is this: we're suffering from a tremendous chasm between what I call catechetics and theology. That is to say, we're still presenting the faith at the level of the instruction of new members and children. At a catechetical level we're doing one thing, and then at the theological level we're doing something very much removed from that. There is a sense in which what we tell our children is really an acid test of what we believe. And it should be. It seems to me that the sort of central simplification which the mystics pursue – the mystic is necessary to theology because he or she is always, or should be, engaged in the process of simplification – is essential. And this uncluttered articulation of faith corresponds to the uncluttered and unapologised-for embodiment of faith. These two things go together: the embodiment of the faith, and the simplicity of articulation. They are the two things necessary if Europe is going to take this on. Otherwise Europe is going to be delivered over to French revolutionary scientific humanism – though it isn't really scientific humanism, it's scientistic humanism. It will give itself out as 'scientific', but because it's not anchored in any finality, it'll be a prey to all sorts of social pressures and manipulations. I think that we're living in the most crucial time since the second century.

And the whole thing about personality and healing has got something to do with this embodiment too, hasn't it? This whole separation of the spirit from the body.

You see, in the sphere of ethics, I think we're in an extraordinary situation. On the one hand we've got, for some reason or other – and this goes right across the denominations – a kind of neurosis about sexuality. Now, since sexuality is a primary part of human existence, we have this awful dilemma. On the one hand, in our own time, we've seen a recrudescence of pretty pagan permissiveness and 'anything goes' in the realm of sexuality – which itself is part of the neurosis. The whole filling of the 'screen' of ethics almost entirely on the sexual front is also part of the neurosis. And yet we can't get over it without devoting a bit of thought and time to this, because the Christian church rightly, it seems to me, has to have some kind of answer to the go-as-you-please stuff. There is a tradition of real ascesis and personal-responsibility stuff within the Christian tradition which can put up some kind of reaction, coming from real faith; and thank God it's done. On the other hand, what we look like in the media, and in most people's minds, is that becoming Christian is immediately to get within this almost *obsessive* preoccupation with the sexual area. Whereas pride, arrogance, theft and greed can be left on the side as minor sins, the whole thing seems to be concentrated now on what you're doing sexually. The very word 'sin' to most people means sexual sin. I think that's true of all our denominations. When you preach about sin, what they're thinking about is sexual aberrations and all the rest of it.

The dilemma is an appalling one because, the more you concentrate on your answer to that, and the thinking of it through, the more you look as if you're neurotically concerned about it. There are times when I would like to have a moratorium on all sexuality problems for about ten years, and get on to targeting a few more ghastly sins which are embodied in society and people. That's not very likely. At other times I think to myself: how do we put up the ethical norm of the humanity of Jesus – always knowing that we've got a bit of a problem here, because Jesus, as a celibate man, doesn't seem in his human condition to be all that helpful about the norm of human existence in this area. I think we all feel this. On the other hand, we daren't take anything else for our ethical norm, because once we move off the humanity of Jesus we're into the field of high relativism and statistics. So, we have a theological difficulty in the realm of ethics: and yet we know it's laid upon us – as Barth would say, and Roman Catholic ethics would say – to talk about the norm of Christ's humanity, which is our norm. We have to, as it were, extrapolate, from the quality of Jesus' love for us all, the quality of love which sexuality can embody. It's a very strange exercise. Isn't that what we're trying to do?

The difficulty here is how the celibate Jesus of the Bible addresses the modern situation.

Paul, of course, rightly takes up part of it. He points out that Christ is the bridegroom of the church, and therefore husband-and-wife relationships are governed, and our human sexual relationships are governed, by that kind of relationship. Well now, that's a beginning. But it's a difficult exercise, and whether we're rigorous or laxist by nature or temperament, what we have to keep in mind through this rather difficult but necessary foundation work is that, to move off from the humanity of Christ, as Barth rightly sees, is to move into a morass of human confusion at this deep level of the sexual. One of the reasons why we're neurotically obsessed is because that is where we're most wounded, perhaps. Because it's about love.

It's the place where we're most vulnerable.

Yes, it's an embodiment of love, and at this very strange and mysterious place in our lives we're all vulnerable at this point. Is that right?

And if it's not tackled at the embodied level, and only becomes a matter of the 'head', we're really in trouble.

Now, can I just speak to you as a Roman Catholic at this point? Because this is what worries me. Very often, the media interpretation of the encyclicals is the one that we all get, both within the church and outside it. They pick on the first bit of what's being said – which is a necessary attempt, whether it comes off or not, to keep the humanity of Christ and the holiness of Christ central to the picture. Now, one can disagree with all sorts of things about the corollaries of all that, but what is distressing to my mind is that the two or three last paragraphs of all those encyclicals are neglected. These are the parts which talk about the compassion and pastoral care that are needed for the human race in the particularities of all this. These things are never mentioned. You've got to have compassion in dealing with people where they are. That bit's always missed out. Even in the posh newspapers, you never see anyone talking about those paragraphs concerning the advice to the pastor. Now, that worries me because it's being made a media hype, which has affected the churches. It's a kind of confrontational thing, and the other bit about how you deal with people in their actual condition is always left out. Nobody says a word about it.

And yet that's where the wounds are.

What we've got to be doing is: on the one hand, keeping the target of Christ's holiness high as high can be, but in pastoral work we need all the tenderness and care to see where a person's at, where he or she can be next, and how the wounds can be healed. I would like a statement to come out which majored on the pastoral side of things, and put where you've got to get to in the *last* two paragraphs! That would be lovely.

It's strange how the whole emphasis on sin goes onto sexual issues, but all the biblical stuff about money and justice somehow becomes very ethereal, very disembodied. In the original tradition, it's not like that at all. You can't read the Bible and get away from stuff about money and the poor, and yet the major emphasis in the church seems to be on sex.

Now, could that be a ducking? There is a bit of a ducking going on whereby the things that would really hurt us to take on board – not that sex is not something that can't hurt us – become privatised into sexuality stuff, and we miss the social dimension. There is a good thing happening in the Catholic Church, which I think is going on apace. Nowadays we have this corporate reconciliation service before the major feasts, where the congregation come for confession. First of all, there is a corporate examination of conscience. I notice very much that there is a high-level application of examining our social sins, corporately done, which is marvellous. And then when we go to confession individually for absolution, the people are already corporately aware of their sins of omission and carelessness about the poor, and all the rest of it. And this is reflected in the confessions they're making. Now that's tremendous, and is really a counterbalance to this sexual preoccupation.

It's a much-needed one, isn't it?

Yes. Because normally speaking, people are obviously highly embarrassed about their sins, but they're more embarrassed about their sexual sins than anything else. It's a big problem for young people coming to confession. The adolescent has already taken on this neurotic preoccupation by the very nature of his condition, and therefore it becomes a huge hurdle which many young people now are falling away from. Whereas if they can see our corporate sins and our sins of carelessness about the human body as belonging together ...

You mean things should get an equal emphasis, not just a question of playing down the sexual side?

Yes, it's the whole range and panorama of our woundedness that's got to come through. Now, would you say that there's a comparable thing going on in sin-consciousness, through the liturgies and worship of other churches?

I think it's more seen in the statements of church bodies, which tend to be very controversial about justice and social matters. I think it tends to be more at that level.

But it wouldn't be sacramentalised in any kind of worship?

No, not very much. But speaking again from the Iona Community side of things which I know, warts and all, it's interesting that another of George MacLeod's campaigns was his pamphlet entitled 'Why the Church of Scotland needs the Confessional' ...

What a lovely title! [*Roland collapses into wheezing laughter.*]

Within the daily liturgy of the Iona Community there is a mutual prayer of confession, so to that degree it's been sacramentalised. And the Community has tended to major on the wider corporate sins. Some people would say that the Community ignores the personal, but I don't think that's true. Nevertheless, it's perceived as being more interested in South America than in what's going on inside the person.

The Iona Community in the 1950s, when I knew it by yearly visits, was for me a tremendous breakthrough, seeing a whole community of people, transmitting all this to group after group on the island. The social implication of sin was not only preached, but daily attended to. I was always moved by the Thursday-evening commitment service, which was really a kind of corporate confessional. You came to terms with yourself and with the wider community. That was always the highlight for me, when we *corporately* did something about it and received a Word chosen from the New Testament. Perfect.

I've just come back from the Easter services on Iona. At the commitment service, the church was packed, and you had about 100 people coming forward. It was as evangelical as any Billy Graham rally. People from all over the world came forward to the communion table, to hear a Word from Jesus. It was very simple and direct and personal. I wish that people who criticise the Community as simply some kind of left-wing pressure group could have been there. They don't understand what it's about.

If I had one desire for the Church in Scotland, it would be for all the churches to take up the possibility of this kind of commitment service. From a Catholic point of view, of course, it doesn't and couldn't replace the absolution, but it would entail a movement among even the most lapsed and careless in a commitment process, with a Word of Christ of forgiveness and acceptance. It can transform whole congregations. I found that at this little Rosslyn Chapel. I used the commitment service there, with everybody saying: 'That was most meaningful'. George MacLeod's prophetic thing was this combination of a personal commitment and the communal embodiment stuff ...

And the healing thing. George kept saying: 'Bodies, bodies, bodies', so much so that his family used to parody him doing this! 'Not again, George!' they'd say. And at Iona the healing service precedes the commitment service. Big numbers of people come forward to receive the ministry of healing. In the main, they're not people with any kind of visible ailment. There's a recognition nowadays that you don't have to be paralysed or leprous before you can come up. You don't even have to feel 'at the end of the line' to need healing.

Oh, it's marvellous. Wonderful. Young people kneeling in the abbey for the laying on of hands. Beautiful. And partly confessional.

Again it's that body thing, isn't it?

Absolutely. You've got to actually move, in the body, up to the Communion rail. For me, these healing and commitment services on Iona are very moving, beyond words. And I think it's a gentle kind of introduction for the priest and minister to the kind of possibility which would reinvigorate congregations, so that they could take part in the necessary embodiment that's going to be. Well, we've got to show it or disappear as effective evangelists.

9

THE ECUMENICAL JOURNEY

How do you see the ecumenical movement, Roland? What should it be about?

I suppose I've lived through all the various stages of ecumenism since the 1930s because I was lucky to have among my teachers people like Father Gabriel Hebert, who was a leader in the Church of England in the realm of ecumenical contacts, especially between the Church of England and the Church of Sweden, of all places. And also he had contacts, which he made me aware of, with people on the Continent like Father Paul Couturier, who I met in 1937 or 1938 when he came to Kelham to talk about Christian unity.

I think it was Paul Couturier who really fired me up for thinking that the visible unity of Christians mattered in presentation of our faith to a divided world. He convinced me that a Church in smithereens, with 240 mainline forms of it, was really a quite useless vehicle for evangelism. That set me thinking about something that still puzzles me – the divisive effect of religion.

We are now going forward with highly pluriform societies, looking for some basic unity which will enable them to live together. By and large, nationalism, racism and religion seem to be the bugbears for finding anything like that. I still think about Paul Couturier and his interpretation of

John's gospel, chapter 17, which was really a Christological interpretation of God's design to bring together people who are scattered abroad. He believed that only a form of Christendom that could be visibly shown to be united, in a diversified pluriformity, could give much hope to the human race. It had to be visible. I remember him stressing this, the *visibility* of unity, so that the world may believe. Couturier was making the point that John 17 was not about some marvellous spiritual bonhomie which can be a friendly toleration of everybody and everything, because the world wouldn't recognise that. It's got to be something so concrete that they can recognise a unity which is a *fact* for them, which they have to take into account.

Well now, my ecumenical progress has been, I suppose, much the same as a lot of people. First of all, I did not only take part in conferences, but also put a lot of faith in meetings of representatives of the different churches. How representative they were, of course, has become more doubtful as the years go on. The first stages of ecumenism, since 1910, were of course these large conferences, giving birth to the World Council of Churches and all the rest of it. And really they were led up to by lots of rather – looking back on it – esoteric conferences of people in the know, or people with ecumenism as a bug. I was in that for quite a long time, and represented the Church of England in the fourfold conversations in Scotland, and all that. Then I think I suffered a change, because I realised that the real differences between Christians were between those who were concerned and involved and those who used the faith – the same faith – as a sort of hot water-bottle and blankets, for cuddling up together, to avoid feeling too cold and out in the rain.

In the 1950s, I was much under the influence of George MacLeod on this one. I found in Iona a kind of ecumenism which suited the stage I was at, because I was realising by then that you could have enormous top-level stuff, and enormous reports which seemed not to get down even onto the minister's table, let alone the tables of the laity. That was the beginning of the ebbing of the tide of interest in ecumenism. And then there was growing up this marvellous finding ourselves shoulder to shoulder with Catholics and Presbyterians – of course I was an Anglican at that time. There was minted then a new kind of ecumenism, which tested itself against political and social things. The prayer life of any community that was involved in this sort of ecumenism was very strong in the 1950s. The Iona prayer disciplines were being taken on not only by the Iona family groups on the mainland, but by ministers and priests who were taking away ideas of common worship and confirmation of faith from the commitment services and the healing services. All this was being spread ecumenically. This lasted, I think, until the 1960s. The 1960s saw a further ebbing of the tide of what I would call formal ecumenism, to the worry and anxiety of some, and perhaps rightfully. The high-up-level conferences were producing less and less fruit at the ground level.

Now we're into the growing of what is called 'grass-roots ecumenism'. Out of all this, two things have come into our little community here. Ecumenism, as I think the Vatican Council saw, couldn't just stop at a domestic movement within the churches. So the Vatican Council gave it a push – which we've had to take up in this house because of contacts with the Vatican – into the wider ecumenism of theism, of Islam and Judaism, and further afield into non-theistic Buddhism. Again you meet the same difficulties. You can land up, if you're not careful, with an esoteric group who are into these things. And they can spend a great deal of time and leisure and their working days on this sort of thing, and meet congenial people who like that sort of thing. So you slowly move into this: how can we have the widest ecumenism, which is about how to get the human race together? This is now the global problem facing politicians. This move, which is fraught with all sorts of bugs of idealism and utopianism, could miss the bus by miles by not heeding the build-up of apocalyptic in the Bible, whereby the horses of division grow as fast as the horses of unity. We have to avoid the kind of easy-going, liberal optimism which believes that the human race is getting more and more unified – which is not so. How does one use what one's learned about dialoguing with people in the domestic situation of the church for this *enormous* width of dialogue with the human being as a human being? This has raised another problem. One of the difficulties of domestic ecumenism in the churches is that they carry this huge baggage of complexity of historical and cultural stuff, which comes to us in a package as Presbyterianism or Anglicanism or Catholicism. In actual fact it's really a rag-bag of a lot of stuff which needs to be sifted before you can really have a proper conversation with your own lot, let alone anyone else.

That's right – just to clear away the debris.

As you go on as a professional ecumenist, you realise that the other bloke is always aware of how much your lot is carrying. The good thing about domestic ecumenism is that we've been made aware, through other people telling us, just how much clutter we carry. Now, let's carry this a stage further – and this is where I nearly disappear out of view with some of this. Buddhism challenges us to get rid of complexity, and I believe the cardinal need of ecumenism – of ourselves one with another – is to work out what is the centrepiece of faith. What is it? Or put it in another rather stark way, what is it we are prepared, or ought to be prepared, to die for? If we ask that of ourselves and of one another, I think we might get somewhere, and not only to come together more closely as Christians. As Christians, I think, we have a duty by virtue of our faith to have such a reformation of clutter that we can go to the world in a simplicity which is overwhelming. Unless this is done, I think domestic ecumenism and the interfaith stuff and the ecumenism of Christians to the rest of the world will lose out. The cardinal point of the coming of Jesus Christ was to cut through the clutter of religion. What we have actually done is to knit together something so complex that you have enormous training programmes before anyone can be admitted.

I remember going to a Buddhist–Christian conference at Amaravati, a Buddhist monastery near London, where I was on the platform with a Buddhist abbot. A girl from the audience asked a good question. She asked the Buddhist abbot: 'When can I become a Buddhist?' He replied like a shot: 'You can begin now'. And there was me thinking of all the complexity of baptism, confirmation, Eucharist and the whole gamut of church initiations. I had to get an answer quickly, because he had answered in one sentence. I said: 'To be a Christian you can begin now, because there is only one thing you have to listen to. You have to listen to a man who says "Follow Me". Next question please!' Now, I came away from that conference thinking to myself: 'How do I put this together?' I gave an answer to that girl which I believe, and yet we have, in all our churches, an enormous amount of esoteric language and stuff to get through before she can really call herself Christian. Now, I don't want to be misunderstood about this, because it involves what Newman calls the development of doctrine. As I understand Newman, one of his tests about the development of doctrine was this: does it cohere with the centrepiece, which is for us the revelation of God the Father in Christ? In what way can we say this so that it's not at all complex, and a child can understand, and a philosopher is never done with it? I believe that this is the only way of going forward.

Clarify it to the essentials?

Yes. What is the root? We can take on board all sorts of things, if they comment on, or give imaginative form, to all that. But what's this root about?

If you were pinned down by the proverbial man in the street who asks: 'What are the essentials?', what would you say? This gets to the heart and core of the thing, doesn't it?

Yes. What is it I want to get over that these blokes from other faiths aren't talking about? What is it I want to get over which the human race doesn't seem to be yet talking about and probably ought to be? What is it that the Christian faith has brought to the human race? I think there are only two unique things in the faith. There are only two. Other things can be paralleled, as we know in comparative religion. The one is the Cross. And the other is the Trinity. Not the *doctrine* of the Cross, but the Cross itself. And not the doctrine of God, but God himself as Trinity. As I understand it, the climax of the radiance of God is paradoxically revealed in a man who's just going to be flung on the scrap-heap of humanity, because this is a demonstration of a love which will go to the limits, and over the limits, in self-giving. It's important not because this is a sort of one-off action of God saying: 'Well, I've got to make this as clear as possible', but because *God is like that*, eternally. The Cross reveals a love in history, which we see is what the whole business of creation is about – an outgoing love which has already been within the Godhead. It's not some monolithic God feeling a bit lonely and wanting something else. The something else has always been within the Godhead, from the Father to the Son and the self-giving Spirit. I mean, it's just incredible. I ask myself almost daily, do I believe in this? I worship relationship. I actually worship relationship. God is love, *is* love – not is loving. He is love, and therefore anybody who abides in this abides in God. And this is the utter simplicity of the relational – a network of relations where existences are determined by relation, not the other way round. And therefore it begins as a kind of philosophy of existence which is much more parallel to the physical world as we know it now, than perhaps we've been able to take on board. You know there's something ecstatic and rational about this.

You're saying that relationship is deeply embedded in the whole of life. It's not an afterthought on God's part: 'I've lived for two million years, and now it's time for relationship'.

No, existence is *like that*. And everything is made and redeemed and sanctified. In fact, sanctification is one long call out into the original image that reflects God. This affects your personal, sexual, political, international life. Prayer is one discipline and loving invitation into this relationship, so that you can establish yourself, so that you can have the guts and energy to work this out in all these other ways. Prayer and all these other sorts of involvement must be held together. They're not options.

So, relationship is at the heart of reality and therefore all other relationships come from this fundamental relationship? That's quite different from the notion of the God who's so different that he's on his own.

Absolutely. God's only kind of transcendence is an upside-down transcendence. It's the transcendence of his eternal and immortal love, which can go down, not up. His transcendence is to get low – in the nativity and the crucifixion. We're seeing a God who can transcend his majesty to come down here. In fact, that's his majesty – that *is* his majesty.

Which turns the whole thing on its head.

Yes. Instead of all this stuff about climbing *up* somewhere to God, in order to get this relational thing with him, we have to go *down* to find him. And we have to go down to find one another. Not up. Going up means a break in relationship. But going down – you find the human as you go down. This is why I'm interested in the movement whereby the gift that can come from the mentally handicapped to the so-called rational is so enormous. The rational ones learn what faith's about by, as it were, coming down to learn from the mentally handicapped. The whole child stuff is all about that. It would be helpful if each tradition was sent away into an ecumenical silence, and they were each asked one question: 'How does your form of tradition as you've received it enable people to take this on board?' Then we would come together, because we would be able to understand why people do this and do that – in pluriformity and diversity, but with a unity of the core. So ecumenism starts with a sign of interest in World Councils and British Councils of Churches, and then comes out into this really paramount question about simplicity.

You're saying that the relationship between the Trinity and the Cross is not some eccentric event. It is actually the heart of the matter because it is the relationship of God with humanity.

And it's gone over the precipice in order to establish it, into hell. He descended into hell: it's terribly important – whether one thinks of it as earthly experience, or whether one takes it overboard and says, yes, even the experience of the nothingness of death, the other side of death. You go as far as you can.

So, simplicity is the fundamental issue here, and it is expressed in the Cross.

If I may just say one thing from my own tradition. In one sense, Catholicism, and the seventeen volumes of the new Catholic encyclopaedia, should give an idea of what it's all about. It's been 'on the ground' all that time and it's a continuous history, and therefore it's a complex history. On the other hand, history also brings us up again and again to the need for simplicity. Catholicism, in one aspect, is the most complex and cluttered form of the Christian faith you could ever imagine. On the other hand, it knows at its heart – and the word 'heart' is important here – that it's got to give focus to centralities. Thinking about two foci of Catholic liturgy and devotion, I would say one is the Mass, which is the sacramental manifestation of this complete self-giving – 'This is my body given for you', taken in such a form that the literalness of the words has to come home each time, so that it's seen to be going on, not just a memory of something else – and the other thing is the Sacred Heart. Now that could end up, and probably very often does, as a pious devotion tacked on to everything else. But in actual fact it is supposed to be the focus of the biblical message of the heart of God. The heart is the focus, the simplicity of human life, the symbol, both in God and man, for the heart of the matter – and as such can be used, and really is meant to be used, as a focus for the simplicity of the Cross. We need to interpret to each other what bits of our tradition are really central to saying all this. Unless they've got straight lines to the centre, I don't know if we need bother too much.

When Karl Barth was asked at a press conference about the meaning of all these volumes of theology he had written, he sang in response: 'Jesus loves me, this I know, for the Bible tells me so'.

Yes! This is all I know, and it's difficult to hang onto that, but this is what faith is teaching me. Everything else – faith's authorities, its ministries, its sacraments – is, as it were, one long service to the centre point. If it isn't, why bother?

The Indian theologian, M. M. Thomas, said that Christianity should be defined by its centre, not by its circumference.

Now, that's exactly it. When you're talking to people of other faiths, or to people without belief, you're thrown back on the question: 'What is it I want to get across? What is it I want to live with?' Not only get across cerebrally, but where is my relational necessity for Christian existence going to express itself in my relationship to him or her?

I suppose that's one of the good things of the ecumenical movement. Because we're being challenged by other people, we have to sit down and attempt to clarify some of these things.

That's right. And that's why I'm not one of those who despise formal ecumenism or think that it's all a dead loss. It's not. It's all been part of a very necessary process in the simplification of faith, so that we can stand up together. And not just stand up together as a kind of religious group, but as one relating to God, related to God, and because of that related to everybody else. We're *there* in Christ, we can't do anything else but relate.

Now, let's just make one thing clear. Some people would say, and rightly, you could end up with a sort of lovey-ducky religion, if love is your centre. That's why the Bible and the mainline tradition of the churches at its most edgy take on board a phrase like the wrath of the Lamb. Because if it's about love, then offences against it, and separations, and unrelational stuff, are condemned to death and nothingness as a judgement – which is worse than just the judgement of anger, it is the judgement of love which has gone to the end. And if, after all that, you still refuse it, then you're in for grave trouble, politically and all the rest of it. So hell is something to take on board. Outside of holy scripture, one of the most inspired sentences is Dante's sign over the gates of hell, 'Eternal love made me'. That was an insight which can't be put aside. You can't go in for a sentimental Jesuology because we worship love. We need the holiness and flaming ruthlessness. I mean, there's something ruthless about the blessed Trinity that you can't muck about with!

And the Cross is the centre of that, though it gets turned into a sentimental object.

The demand of the Cross and the grace of the Cross, going hand in hand, are the most terrifying things you're likely to experience in life. Fire is one image of God, and fire is a very dangerous thing to muck about with. I would want to challenge the kind of easy liberalism of some of our ecumenical activities, as if we're joining together our wetness rather than our strength. There's a kind of wet, liberal, undemanding, easy-going muck that can be the very reverse of all this.

It becomes 'It's nice to be nice'.

I remember old Father Kelly used to say to us: 'They've changed those words of St John, "God is light, and in him is no darkness at all". They've changed it to "God is nice, and in him is no nastiness at all"!' The first sort of reaction of some people is to say: 'Oh well, you know, you can end up with the kind of gentle Jesus, meek and mild stuff, which is the very opposite of the truth'. Conservatives are right to give an edge to this, and liberals are wrong. That's why I'm a radical, but I'm not a liberal.

I'm intrigued that you chose the Trinity when focusing on simplicity. A lot of theologians would say that the Trinity is one of the complicating, complex things, rather than the simplifying things. How do you respond to that?

I would go so far as to say that I would bring a child up on the Trinity. A priest at Millport who spent two hours a week teaching the kids at a secular school came to me one morning, having been at the school. He said: 'I must tell you this. I was giving the eight-year-olds a lesson and I said to them that one day, perhaps in a couple of years' time, I'd be talking to them about the God as Trinity, but of course they weren't ready for that. A hand shot up. 'Yes, Tommy.' 'I know all about the Trinity', said Tommy. 'Oh you do, do you – well you better come and tell the class all about it.' So Tommy came to the front: 'Well, there's God you see, and there's the Father, the Son and the Holy Spirit and they love one another so much that they're one'. And he went and sat down.

What else is there to say?

I would begin with relational stuff with kids, and not be like Schleiermacher, who really put the Blessed Trinity as a *possible* model, as an *appendix* to normal Christian faith. And that's where the rot sets in.

A wee optional extra.

I feel that all these words about the 'majesty' and the 'glory' of God have got to be crucified. One of the difficulties for us is that, in the creed, we acknowledge, as logically we have to acknowledge, the almightiness of God, and we have to talk about the crucifixion in the middle of it. In actual fact, 'And crucified under Pontius Pilate' has to be the centrepiece from which you interpret the word 'almighty'.

That's the only way the almightiness of God can be properly understood?

Yes, otherwise we think he is a sort of Shah of Persia, up to the *n*th degree, a way of talking about God as being mightier than we can even conceive a man. Then you're in grave trouble. But the almightiness of God is in his love, having made everything seen and unseen.

I remember listening to a tape of yours, in which you complained about Paul being interpreted fairly juridically, and you argued the need to restate it all in terms of the personal. Is that part of what you're saying here about relationships?

Yes, Paul's purple passages are when he is free of his rabbinical arguments or his juridical stuff. The passages that everybody quotes and reads again and again are the ones in which he is personal about 'Christ Jesus, who loved me and gave himself to me'. Or 'Who shall separate us from the love of God that we have in Christ Jesus our Lord?' Once he's got that, he's away. That's what keeps him in the canon of scripture, it seems to me, those tremendous breakthroughs from his more unconverted rabbinism. Well, first-century rabbinism. After all's said and done, we mustn't condemn rabbinism, because most Christian ministers have trained themselves into being rabbis anyway. There is a sense in which you've got to work out, at all sorts of levels of moral counsel and even casuistry, how this love works out. But if you lose the point on the way to doing that, then you're back into the disease of all religion.

You mentioned the Bible, and people returning to the Bible. And another pattern over this period has been the rediscovery of the Bible within the Roman communion, and correspondingly the rediscovery of sacramental life within the Presbyterian communion. Have you observed that?

In the Scottish scene, I would wish there was a bit more knowledge of what the others are doing. One of the things that impedes a progress of union of mind and heart, and eventually some kind of visible communion between Christians, is the fact that we haven't learned to take on, and be responsible for, and know something about, our neighbours. One of the things we are able to do here, in a small, thimbleful kind of way, is just to be a little place which is not so big and so organised and so obviously anything, in a little hut chapel, that people can come to us without fear. In doing so, they discover that the Catholic Mass is full of scripture readings and at most of the Masses a diligent priest can and very often does preach a little sermon about the gospel of the day. This is unknown to the majority of non-Catholic Scots. And similarly we found the other way round: there are many Catholics who come here to an Anglican Eucharist on the day we celebrate non-

Catholic Mass, and again it is the first time they've ever been to an Anglican Eucharist. They say: 'It's almost the same as ours!' as they go out. So all this information and experience of one another's thing has got to go on before we can reap the benefit of these two movements – the Bible in the Catholic Church and the new sacramental experience of non-Catholics. Though one must say of the Episcopal Church in Scotland that almost its sole *raison d'être* has been to be a non-Catholic form of sacramental Christianity.

Or perhaps a non-Roman, Catholic Church.

Yes. As they would say. And that's got to be respected, because through thick and thin they did preserve that sacramental tradition, in face of a highly non-sacramental church. Though one mustn't go too far, because the Church of Scotland has preserved an incredible faithfulness to the fact that the Eucharist is the gathering of everybody. So their communions four times a year are still something, as in this village. They are communion days when the whole village knows that it's communion Sunday.

The preparation for it: communion cards being put through people's doors – it's a big event.

And it seems to me that the two traditions of the multiplication of the daily Masses in the Catholic sense and the weekly communions of the Episcopalians have to take on board, and respect, highly respect, this very Catholic feel of the corporate totality of Christian believers in the communion service of the Church of Scotland. We're very far from respecting one another's practices at present, I would say. Are we?

And this is largely ignorance, you feel.

Ignorance, partly because many people have never been to a Church of Scotland celebration. And I would say, to anybody in Scotland if they want to see that, and see it done weekly, the best place to go is Iona, where the Iona Community has been more instrumental than any other group of people, I think, in bringing back this ability to combine the totality of Eucharist with weekly celebration. That's a very effective instrument of ecumenism in Scotland.

What would you say now, as a priest of the Roman communion, about the Church of Scotland communion service? After all, theologically it is still very far from being the sacrifice of the Mass.

Well, yes and no. You see, here's an extraordinary thing. When I first came to Scotland, I was put on to the Conversations between the Church of England and the Church of Scotland. And some of the high, Anglo-Catholic Anglicans in the commission were very worried about this whole business of whether the Church of Scotland could ever take on board the sacrificial aspect of the Eucharist. And I discovered, when I was having to prepare a little thing about all this for them, that the Church of Scotland in its liturgy – which of course is not *de rigueur*: it's put out by the committee of the Assembly for devotion, therefore it hasn't got the liturgical rigour of an ordered rite that has to be used anyway, like either the Anglicans or the Roman Catholics have – nevertheless, in the traditional rite of the Church of Scotland, these words come immediately after the words of consecration: 'We plead before you the one sacrifice of Christ'. Now, to plead before the Father the one sacrifice of Christ seems to be an eminently reasonable, succinct statement of what the sacrifice of the Mass is. It's exactly what we do. We're pleading one sacrifice, now in time and space for us in this service, which was once for all offered by Christ in his death on Calvary, and is eternally offered in the heavens. It seems to me that that is far in advance of the Zwinglian Book of Common Prayer rite of Cranmer in 1662.

So, you're saying that they have moved?

Well, I don't know if they've ever not moved, from the point of view of what they're able to *say*.

Are you then saying that all the arguments and discussions between Contarini and Melanchthon and Luther about the sacrifice, and the efficacy of the sacrifice, were insignificant and so much playing with words?

No, I don't think I could say that. But I think that in the issues round how you speak – because we've all got this difficulty, Catholic as well as non-Catholic – we've always got this perennial difficulty of harmonising, bringing into play, three factors in the one sacrifice of Christ. The sacrifice is, on the one hand, offered once and for all, completely and without remainder, by the death of Christ, and he was the offerer on Good Friday. On the other hand, Calvin would be the first to acknowledge, and couldn't do otherwise, with the Epistle to the Hebrews in his Bible – and I think this is true of Luther – that the sacrifice of Christ is an eternal sacrifice: that is to say, it is always before the Father's face. In one sense, it was a lamb slain before the foundation of the world – it was from beginning to end of time, and at the end the lamb stands as the centre of the worship of heaven. So, from the beginning of Genesis to the end of the Bible, it's about a sacrifice of a lamb, an immaculate innocent lamb – of a son in the Abraham story – but it's always been, as it were, woven into the very pristine and final relationship of ourselves to God. There's that.

Well now, what's the relationship between the eternal sacrifice in heaven, shown once and for all in its completeness in Christ, and the sacramental bringing-in to our presence, in the Eucharist, of the sacrifice of Good Friday and the eternal sacrifice in heaven? I think that with the Contarini/Luther/Calvin debate that was going on at the Reformation, they each of them found it hard to say how they saw it, because the Catholics had dented their own doctrine by a mathematical, almost account-book idea of Masses – as if thirty was better than one, and it had become almost a commercial transaction between God and man, that man made for his part either by saying the Mass or paying for the Mass. On the other hand, the Reformers themselves were so clear that the main plank of their reform was to restore the communion to the people that their emphasis on the communion as the Eucharistic climax made it almost impossible for them to find the room that they could have done for a kind of sacrificial aspect. So, in a way, the sixteenth century is not very helpful to us. We have to look at all this again, because things are much more fluid. The Evangelical who takes Toplady's hymn and sings: 'Nothing in my hand I bring, simply to thy cross I cling' is really saying, from his interior faith disposition, what the whole Church is saying when we go to Mass. That's all we can offer; we haven't got anything else.

So there are possibilities in the Scottish scene, but I think the trouble is we haven't got enough experience of one another. I'm always trying to give people the courage to experience what Vatican II has asked Catholics to do – to experience the worship of the non-Catholic, and vice versa.

10

CAMPING OUT IN SUBURBIA

*(A conversation with Roland Walls and
Brother John Halsey)*

JOHN: Roland, you've gone all over the world on your little thing about 'Return empty to Roslin'. That's an extraordinary story.

And funny. It's a very funny story.

ROLAND: Yes, but also people think you're crazy. You tell that to a lot of clergymen, why you're in the town. Eh? A British Rail notice! Return empty to Scotland! Is that right? But it's all crazy stuff, isn't it?

Yes, and there has to be a kind of craziness in people to listen to that.

ROLAND: Oh yes. If you haven't got any craziness, you write it off. It's offensive. Isn't it?

JOHN: And the curious thing is, although that was long before the Community, and long before I thought about it at all, it's the reason why I'm here. Why is the Community at Roslin? Well, in a sense, that's the reason. And that's got implications, you know!

ROLAND: But what was going to come out of that, except just a command? Return. Empty. That's all there was. There was nothing to say what was going to happen.

But God's never like that, is he?

ROLAND: Never! You don't know his will until you've done it.

What's that line in Newman's hymn ...

ALL: 'I do not ask to see the distant scene, one step enough for me.'

ROLAND: Exactly, that's the thing. Old Father Kelly used to say: 'Oh Lord, I think I know the distant scene, it's the next step I don't know anything about!' [*Wheezes with laughter.*] Kelly was a funny man, wasn't he! I think I get a lot from Kelly, don't I?

JOHN: Yes. That's another load of stories, which ought to be on tape. Like Roland's first lesson in theology, which we heard him relaying to some sisters last Sunday, when we were having lunch with them.

ROLAND: The first lesson in systematic theology was going to be given by Father Kelly at five o' clock on a nice afternoon in September 1936.

This is Father Kelly of the Society of the Sacred Mission?

ROLAND: Yes, the founder. I was coming up from what would be known as the junior seminary to the senior seminary, and beginning theology proper. So my Auntie Nellie had bought me a new copy of the Revised Version of the Bible, and a fountain pen, and a lovely exercise book, I can see it now. And I'd headed it all: 'Systematic theology, Lecture 1, Father Kelly SSM'. The old man came in, aged – well, he was about 70, I suppose. He says: 'Ooh Lord', he says, 'You can't think about God closed up in a room. Let's get out into his universe!' So he led us all out, all twenty of us, through some French windows, into the flower garden, across the cricket pitch and football pitches, until we got to the cabbage patch;

then through the cabbage patch, until we landed up at the pigsties. There was an old sow in there, sunning herself in the September sunlight, and old Kelly said to us: 'Now sonnies, look at that old sow'. So we looked at it for five minutes, and nothing said by him; we made a lot of ribald remarks, but he just let us look on. Then he said: 'Now, God has either everything to do with that old sow, or he's got nothing to do with anything in this world. You may go.' First lesson. We were sacristy rats, you see. All of us were sacristy rats. We thought God was candles and Bibles and novenas, and goodness-knows-what.

So he was rubbing your face in the Incarnation.

ROLAND: Exactly.

JOHN: Another thing about old Kelly I remember you saying was that he was bed-ridden for his last few years, and Roland was looking after him. This was at a later stage, when Roland was a novice. And there are all sorts of stories about that actually! But one thing was that he had an L-plate on his mantelpiece.

ROLAND: He was a learner to the end of his life.

JOHN: This was the founder of a marvellous religious community.

ROLAND: And when he died, we don't know what his last words were. It's typical old Kelly. He muttered in his delirium, and we thought he said he wanted Bass every day. We didn't know whether it was Mass or Bass. So we gave him both. He was having a bottle of Bass every day and Mass every day! We still don't know! Isn't that beautiful?

So there it is. You see, it is marvellous to be born mad, because you pick up things that people don't, if they're not mad. I'm sure madness is a sixth sense, a fourth dimension. Is it?

I'm just struggling with your use of the word 'mad'.

ROLAND: Well, 'mad' means non-rational at least, and very occasionally irrational.

JOHN: Yes, it's being open to another dimension, isn't it?

ROLAND: Going beyond logic and structures and everything else.

Yes, well, I think it's being alive to the Spirit and to a set of values that aren't ...

ROLAND: But putting it that way looks like a virtue, whereas this is not a virtue, it's something you're cursed with or blessed with.

Roland mentioned this morning how the business of monasticism is clearing away all the normal controls which govern your life – finance, family, commitments, mortgage and so on. Clear all that out of the way and you create an empty space, and that's why rules are important in monasticism, because you've got to clear a space and keep it.

JOHN: Yes, they're sort of negatively important.

Yes, that's right. And then into that space, God brings all sorts of seemingly chaotic ...

JOHN: Yes, and other people bring all sorts of stuff too. It's a messed space, actually! But you have to have faith in that space.

It's a mess only in the sense that it doesn't conform to our ideas of order.

ROLAND: That's right. The temptation is to try and move in.

JOHN: But it's not only God who brings things into that space. All sorts of funny things come up from one's own murky depths – and crap from local society and the world. It gets covered with shite.

ROLAND: Well, yes, the world throws shite into it.

JOHN: And we have to keep on clearing the space! And listening in faith that God is speaking there too.

ROLAND: God brings his own goodness. But the world and ourselves, all we can throw in is our own rot.

When you say that the world throws in a lot of shite, can you give us some examples of what you mean by that?

JOHN: People come to the house, because we've got space, with situations which are quite beyond them or us to do anything about. That's one aspect of it.

ROLAND: We get people who come to control us, sinister people. That can happen. Really sinister manipulation.

JOHN: With great power. And sometimes the communications people, the press and television, all this sort of thing.

ROLAND: But also the people themselves. Need can bring a lot of evil into the world. You feel as if other people want that space. Or another spirit wants that space.

JOHN: It has a peculiar dynamic, this space, doesn't it?

ROLAND: Yes, if you create an empty space, it's dangerous in a way, because it can be filled negatively or positively. And you feel always precarious.

So you've got to do a lot of clearing out. I suppose sometimes you're telling people to go?

ROLAND: Yes. And telling ourselves. It comes from us.

JOHN: But on the other hand, always being ready to receive people as well. It's an odd business.

ROLAND: It's all very odd. It's all crazy. But how can you get anybody to see that, as a vocation? I find, looking at it, looking at my own life, I think to myself, well it's all so odd. You can't expect anybody to see it easily. I can't, sometimes. It's not obvious, is it, that it's a thing to do!

No, it's very much something which is discovered.

JOHN: Perhaps it isn't our job to see it. Perhaps our job is just to be obedient to Jesus.

ROLAND: I'm sure that's right, but there is a sense in which you do want what you've seen to be seen by somebody else.

Oh yes, that's a natural thing. But you see now, some of the greatest saints we've got, including Our Lord himself, are very rude people from time to time. Saint John the Baptist was very rude. St Francis was rude. And that rudeness doesn't come from any natural arrogance or anything like that; it comes actually from profound humility, doesn't it, which gives them the power to ...

ROLAND: Yes, because they've got nothing to gain or lose by what they're doing.

It gives them a power to identify something which is invading, or manipulative.

ROLAND: Oh yes.

And tell it to ...

ROLAND: Go! Well, we've found very often that we've got to shore ourselves up on that side, because the natural tendency of gospel-readers is to become rather flabby ...

... and nice.

ROLAND: Nice. That comes back to old Kelly. Kelly used to say: 'The most disastrous thing in Christian history is to translate a word from Saint John into its own language:

"God is nice, and in him is no nastiness at all"! But "God is light, and in him there is no darkness at all" is quite a different thing.' I think the business of being nice to people can throw us again and again. From time to time, we have to make quite sure we're not sliding into that kind of nonsense. It's very odd stuff, isn't it? But you get the temptation to think that you could be on the wrong tack. Your only confirmation about this is that something happens from time to time. But there are times when I think to myself, in the small hours of the morning, I get terrified that we're proud of all the wrong things, that we ought to be doing what everybody else is doing!

JOHN: As we've gone on, we've noticed the changes. This place sticks out more and more like a sore thumb as the years go by; one time it looked like a piece of nonsense, but now it fits into things less and less, doesn't it, as the world changes. And we change too, actually, but we change in the opposite direction.

ROLAND: It's like camping out, isn't it? Like a hippy encampment really. It is like camping out in the middle of suburbia!

JOHN: And you can never make plans about where you ought to be moving towards.

Roland: How can you convey that? Perhaps John's right, you just can't do it. For example, you've just got to do it and it'll all fold up when it's gone.

JOHN: Yes, I think leave it to the Lord.

ROLAND: Well, we can't do anything else! And this is another feeling – perhaps it's only me, but I think it's true of all of us: you feel trapped. The thing is a trap. I think it's the Lord's trap, but you're trapped. You can't do anything about it.

JOHN: Yes, one aspect of that is that if this thing folded up now – if Roland, say, went under a bus or what-have-you, and I was pushed into the big wide world – I mean, you're fit for nothing after this. I don't see how I could be what I was trained to be, a parish priest; any training one has had has been unpicked. I am fit for nothing else but life here and now. And that's a bit frightening. And it's frightening especially when we take on – for instance, receiving Jonathan's life vows – responsibility for a life which has no future. Obviously one only does this because Jonathan knows, and we know, that our only future is with the Lord, and that's understood; but then there are more immediate responsibilities –

Yes, I can understand the feeling of fear there.

ROLAND: Oh yes, there's a fear.

Loss of freedom?

ROLAND: Yes, we're trapped, there's nothing we can do.

Does this community have any reserves? Life insurance?

JOHN: No, we set our faces against that. We have said that the gospel enjoins us to take no thought for the morrow.

ROLAND: So we throw away, except for a monthly dilapidations thing.

JOHN: So we're responsible, in the fact that we fulfil the legal requirements; we have insurance for the house.

ROLAND: We pay stamps. But we haven't got any cushion, you see.

JOHN: We don't have any investments.

ROLAND: We can't move. You can't do anything if you haven't got any money. You're the poor, you haven't got any choice. That's the trap. It's an economic trap as well as a trap about your capacity to do things. Because if you get trained into this let-it-all-happen stuff, you are untraining yourself for any job; you can't do both – remain a competent citizen, or a competent churchman, or a competent anything! So you're unpicking as fast as you're doing the other one ...

This is St Peter leaving his boat behind.

JOHN: In a way, yes. But it's never comfortable.

ROLAND: There's a certain element of fear all the time. Deep down. Sometimes when you're on a retreat or something on your own, these are the kind of things that come up and hit you – that you're not really about serving the Lord without fear, not completely without fear, because you've still got this little worry ...

Your friends worry about this aspect of your life as well. We worry about the cold for you, and we worry about the discomfort, and we worry about the future, and we have never known exactly what to do with that worry; because we know that any approach to say: 'Do you want any help, or financial cushion or anything like that?' would be inappropriate. And yet we don't know what's going to happen to you all!

ROLAND: It's nice to think we've got friends who think like that, but on the other hand, as you say, if we did start thinking about it, it wouldn't be this, would it? So, while it lasts, it's got to be like that. One of the reasons we decided to come under the Benedictine Rule was for Jonathan's sake. Say he was, because of his age, left behind and nobody else was here, then the church authorities could get a transfer for him to a Benedictine place, because he's taken his vows according to the rule. So there's a bit of a safety net there, which we, the older ones, are responsible for providing Jonathan with. It's the least we could do, to make it quite clear that he could live out the rest of his life under the vows – so that his lifelong taking of vows wasn't a meaningless thing in the sense that there was some way in which he could do it, even though it wouldn't be the same kind of thing as this. In fact, I think it would be very painful, to have to join a rather ...

JOHN: That's part of the trap, isn't it? For instance, there's almost nothing like this which is ecumenical. I couldn't see myself as part of something which was denominational.

ROLAND: We've lived outside that for so long. Our life together has proved you can live the Christian life at the level of real unity.

JOHN: And this is where we need to be. Part of the riches of this place comes from being ecumenical.

ROLAND: Though not in a very ecclesiastical way, is it? It's just by people bumping into us, from Plymouth Brethren or nothing at all ...

JOHN: And one notices how impoverished life within a denomination would be by comparison.

ROLAND: You don't come up against that awful business of where the churches are. We have to live where the churches are, with our communion discipline, but it contradicts everything we're living, you see. So we have this awful pain of dislocation at the very centre of our lives, yet in actual living of the life we can be completely one, and we always are. We're not allowed to vote, for example. We don't vote about anything.

Within your community.

ROLAND: Yes. We just get together and there's a common mind. It's amazing how the common mind does appear.

We've never been even tempted to put anything to the vote, have we? And it would be completely against everything we think, to vote. You wait until there's a common mind, then you talk about it, and it's obvious what we're all going to do. About details or big things. But you can't convey that to people who are in a different situation. It's this business of not being able to convey, which I think is really painful. I find this the hardest of all. You can go and tell people about it, but …

Did it occur to you, when you were choosing the name of this community, the Transfiguration, that you are – and it's painful to say this – a temporary sign on earth which, like the Transfiguration, appears and reveals glory, and then stops? And when it stops, there is no institution carrying on?

ROLAND: No. There's no way of carrying us on. There's no way.

JOHN: I'd thought of the Transfiguration earlier, when we were talking about getting Roland on tape; in a sense, the disciples wanted to get it 'on tape', didn't they? 'Lord, it is good for us to be here.' We want to keep this moment. Let's …

Let's box it up.

JOHN: Yes.

ROLAND: It's not possible.

JOHN: You can't do that.

ROLAND: Still the Transfiguration thing moves me, I think because of three reasons. One: Taizé. I was there three or four months before we began this, and I learnt that the Transfiguration mystery for a community is a very positive and enriching thing. And they chose that as their dedication. They don't often speak about it, but it is there. The second thing was that we'd learnt an awful lot through eastern spirituality stuff, and the Transfiguration for them is as important as Christmas and Pentecost. And lastly, the atom bomb was the most horrifying, dehumanising thing. It fell on the feast of the Transfiguration, which was the glorification of humanity! So we chose that. But on the way to it, one of the things we've discovered about here, which we're very conscious of, is that the very buildings we live in – the huts, the chapel – everything is highly impermanent. It will fall into the ground, there won't be any trace of anything that we are. There's nothing here that's permanent. Which is good. So we're doomed.

Painful to realise, but salutary.

ROLAND: Good heavens, terrible – in one sense – that it's transitory. But as you say, there's no guarantee that anybody can continue this for ever and ever. Nor is there any point in it, in a funny sort of way. That makes it hard to introduce life profession into something transitory. It demands life profession; and yet it can't be ever guaranteed in the form that you actually enter. Because when you get to that point, we can't guarantee security to anybody.

JOHN: It's insecurity, and it's also to do with the poor, I think. We continually discover more about the Transfiguration as we go along, don't we? And this came, interestingly, clear to me on the occasion when we first made contact with L'Arche, and I was asked to go up and speak to a big conference they had in Inverness. And so I did my little spiel, which was really about this place and working in a garage, and prayer and involvement; and then after I'd done my speech, my little spiel, there was a question: why do you call yourselves the Community of the Transfiguration? And I found myself talking about what Roland talked about, but in terms of this generation, the human race at this point of time being faced with this question mark: which way are we going to go? And you either go the way of the world and power and wealth and security, and defending your security, and into armaments, and that way goes to the bomb; or you go the other way, with Jesus, who ties himself up with the poor, and takes on their futurelessness. That's his future, with the poor. And that goes to the Cross. And that is the way to glory and transfiguration. So you've got disfiguration or transfiguration. And this rang bells with L'Arche, because that's their way as well, with the 'poor'.

ROLAND: They've got no future, no choices, the mentally handicapped. It's the same sort of thing. They haven't got any security, anything. Poor old dears. Except what anybody gives them.

Where I think we need to work something out is this: many friends of ours, you and many more, they come and say: 'We see something in all this; now, how do we get on with that out there? How do we translate this into the ordinary living of a job, and a family, and a house, and all the worries and anxieties one has about living at all responsibly in society: how do we do that?'

Well now, we've had many, many attempts. Our own Rule has it: we daren't live here without being open to other people who wish to live under this spirit. It's in the Rule. Well now, the latest we've done about that is what we call Tabor Houses. Tabor Houses are houses where the whole business of contemplative prayer, availability to people without label, and a kind of make-do-and-mend within the reasonableness of their job and family needs and all the rest of it, can be worked out – but where it means also, physically, there is either a room or a corner which is really the reminder of the paramountcy of the kingdom of God: a prayer corner or a chapel or something which corresponds to a piece of floor for a poor man, expressing that kind of availability to God and to man. Now, Tabor Houses: how many have we got, now? We don't know, because they keep spreading. They're not tied to this house, because if people see something in that, they can go and do another one. But it's very difficult to put this out in a packaged form for people in lay, married or secular life of some kind. But we are sure that our function within the church, as with all these other places, is to the committed lay life, the lay married life, that's going to make a difference to the Christian's presence in the world – not just these one-off things. That's important to us. That's why we need the people who come to this house, with that ability to pick up on the pores, the essence of this place, and to say to oneself: 'Yes. Good. There's something there. Okay. How do we do our own translation – which we can't do for you – and do that authentically enough to say, yes, we are part of this scene and linked to all sorts of other things that are going on like this?' Is that right?

POSTSCRIPT:
A 'CHEEKY' SERMON

This sermon was preached by Roland Walls at the con-secration of two friends as bishops in St Paul's Cathedral on 30 September 1980. 'That's the cheekiest thing I ever said', he proudly told Brother John Halsey. 'It's a great gift to be cheeky at the right place and moment.' He was referring in particular to the sentence 'An Anglican bishop is as much an absurdity as an Anglican Bible, an Anglican creed or an Anglican sacrament'. The date is significant – a year before he was received into the Roman Catholic Church. Roland would not have felt able to say what he did as a Roman Catholic.

In their reflection together on the sermon, Brother John reminded Roland of some advice the revered Father Jock Dalrymple had given him about not being cheeky as a Roman Catholic priest. He said that on ordination it was as if you were given a peashooter with just five dry peas for ammunition. It was no good trying to use them to sink a battleship, but if a pompous prelate came into one's sights, one shouldn't miss the opportunity.

There is an amusing side story to the main event. When Roland arrived at St Paul's Cathedral, the man on the door tried to turn away this apparent tramp, saying that an 'important service' was about to begin. He was disconcerted, to say the least, when the 'dosser' explained that he was the preacher.

A CONSECRATION SERMON

Jesus said to Peter: 'Feed my sheep' and when he had spoken this he said 'Follow me' (John 21:17, 19)

Five words of Jesus spoken after breakfast on an April morning give continuity and substance to what is done today, for all the distance of time and the sophistication of tradition.

So, were we right to be embarrassed when the Scottish minister of our parish brought along to our religious community a young man called Angus? He had asked the minister in post-Christian innocence whether what he saw in the television film *Jesus of Nazareth* still went on, because he would like to join it. The minister invited him to his parish church, and we invited him to stay a day with us, but we all knew very well that both the parish and ourselves were rather too far a cry from the original for Angus to see immediately any identity. We were embarrassed. After all, he had been moved week by week, at the sight of twelve bewildered men as they listened to words whose pennies didn't drop until it was too late. He had been watching these men keep company with someone who revealed who he was and who his Father was, by walking ahead of them into other people's disasters, into other people's joys, and therefore to his own disaster and his own final joy. Each of them felt a perfect fool in Christ's company and often acted like one. Each of them discovered in themselves the breaking point of denial and betrayal. In fact, it was just at Peter's painful remembering of his weakness (when Jesus asked the question the dreadful third time: 'Do you love me?') that he was forgiven and commissioned to care for that man's sheep, and asked to start following again. Is it all really still going on? 'Of course', we would like to say; but it's not always obvious, and we were embarrassed.

In spite of the overlay of things done 'decently and in order', we would want Angus to see and hear today what he saw on television – to see the same Christ giving his commission to our two brothers Keith and Eric to feed the sheep and to still keep following – to follow Christ in his compassionate attention to the crowd, the sheep of the first three gospels as well as the more exclusive churchly sheep of St John's gospel – that unshepherded crowd of people of our own nation 'scattered like sheep on a cloudy and dark day' – to follow Christ by attending to and spending time with the professedly non-religious, those who do not belong to the various clubs of economic, social and religious security; indeed, for some of whom social security will never mean more than a subsistence allowance from the state.

We do our apostolic men, our bishops, grave harm when we expect them to serve the self-satisfaction of a decayed and disappearing Christendom, when we see them as a couple more VIPs to grace our ecclesiastical and social occasions, to satisfy our craving for position and presence, and to assure the survival of our favourite religious club. Christ would have none of it. He turned his attention away from the influential to the common man. He was found among men and women without a future, among the dispossessed of the earth. He used the occasions when he did dine out to be rather unpleasant to his host. He was a great disappointment to those who expected him to bolster up the religious and political scheme as he found it. No, he walked to his Father through the crowds of unacceptables and reached the zenith of his love and obedience by dying among the very riff-raff.

We need to look below and beyond the trimmings of vestment and place today and pray for two men who are entering into an ambiguous leadership in which they will have to disappoint many hopes if they are to follow Christ, that great shepherd of the sheep. For the church of this nation has not yet made up its mind whether it is the tail end of a vanishing Christendom or the cold-footed follower of Jesus Christ.

I have little doubt as to the answer in the hearts of these two friends of ours today. It is to serve and follow Jesus.

This Lord of ours is replacing the stained-glass, brass-rubbed image of a bishop with the icon of the careworn face of Helder Camara, the shattered face of Archbishop Romero, the corpse of Archbishop Luwum. These are men who, dead or alive, 'preach not themselves but Christ Jesus as Lord and themselves as our servants for Jesus' sake'. These are men who have dared to go upstream against the flow of influential opinion, who plead the cause of the poor and exploited. Their terrible voices are heard after the complacent pieties of the tamed pulpit have died on our ears. 'Dramatic exceptions', you may say. Maybe – but also dramatic indications of a sea-change which the church of our nation cannot evade. Neither she nor her servants dare succumb at this hour to the snares of popularity and acceptability.

My brothers, my very dear friends, Keith and Eric, against all odds your wish today is to affirm your desire to be numbered among the apostles, with all that that entails of bewilderment and repeated inability to follow a patient and exacting Christ. You are fully aware in the Spirit that this must be no inauguration of two managers of a religious club. You are aware, too, that you must overcome in your lives the contradiction of being a denominational bishop. An Anglican bishop is as much an absurdity as an Anglican Bible, an Anglican Creed or an Anglican Sacrament.

You don't need my words to tell you of the hunger we have to meet men of God, not any more churchmen – but men of God who by daily assiduous prayer and study of the Scriptures come from God to be living icons of God the Father. Our presence here on this happy day will mean something to us all if we join you in deep prayer that you will be given the courage to say a firm 'No' to those who require you to see your office in any other light than that of the gospel, be they never so grand, or the occasion, in the eyes of the world, never so important. We pray that you have the courage to say 'No' to all who will nibble your life away in ecclesiastical bureaucracy which still proliferates its suffocation of the Spirit. We pray you will have courage to say 'Yes' to all who are in need – to have 'a special care for the outcast and needy', as the new rite so movingly puts it, to say 'Yes' to all chances to lead a frightened, timid church out in a boldness not its own to come to the help of the fear-ridden lives of dying men; men who live without God and without hope under the threat of the unthinkable, diabolic obscenity of technological war. We pray that you will say 'Yes' to any request to help people pray to their Father in secret as well as at church services – to say 'Yes' to any opportunity given you to put right the most terrible indictment of a contemporary prayerless Christianity – its failure to divert a thirsty generation of the young to the depths of the prayer of Christ.

Under such leadership, we would hope with less embarrassment to direct Angus who asked the question 'Where is it all today?' to the authentic apostolic succession of these who follow Jesus in responsible, obedient, burden-bearing groups – apostles themselves indeed who in their weakness and insignificance make possible the miracle of God. For by a few poor men in every place he may yet save the cities of this world.